THE 20-MINUTE BREAK

OTHER BOOKS BY ERNEST LAWRENCE ROSSI

Dreams and the Growth of Personality

The Psychobiology of Mind-Body Healing: New Concepts of Therapeutic Hypnosis

The February Man: Evolving Consciousness and Identity in Hypnotherapy (with Milton Erickson)

Experiencing Hypnosis: Therapeutic Approaches to Altered States (with Milton Erickson)

Hypnotherapy: An Exploratory Casebook (with Milton Erickson)

Hypnotic Realities (with Milton Erickson)

Mind-Body Therapy: Ideodynamic Healing in Hypnosis (with D. Cheek)

THE 20-MINUTE BREAK

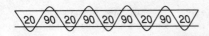

Reduce Stress, Maximize Performance, and Improve Health and Emotional Well-Being Using the New Science of Ultradian Rhythms

ERNEST LAWRENCE ROSSI, Ph.D.
with DAVID NIMMONS

JEREMY P. TARCHER, INC.
Los Angeles

Library of Congress Cataloging-in-Publication Data

Rossi, Ernest Lawrence.
    The 20-minute break: reduce stress, maximize performance, and improve
health and emotional well-being using the new science of ultradian rhythms /
by Ernest Lawrence Rossi with David Nimmons.
        p. cm.
    Includes bibliographical references.
    ISBN 0-87477-585-X : $17.95
    1. Stress management.   2. Ultradian rhythms.   I. Nimmons, David.
II. Title.   III. Title: Twenty-minute break.
RA785.R674   1991   91-10698
155.9 ' 042—dc20   CIP

The list on page 117–119 is courtesy of Elizabeth Kaufmann, ©1989 by Elizabeth Kaufmann, and reprinted with permission. The tables on pages 23 and
58 are courtesy of *Psychological Perspectives* (Fall 1990).

Jeremy P. Tarcher, Inc.
5858 Wilshire Blvd., Suite 200
Los Angeles, CA 90036

Distributed by St. Martin's Press, New York

Design by Tanya Maiboroda

Manufactured in the United States of America
10   9   8   7   6   5   4   3   2   1

First Edition

CONTENTS

Prologue   VII

1. On the Trail of a Scientific Mystery   I

2. The Mind–Body Rhythms of Self-Regulation   14

3. Stressing Out:
   When Ultradian Rhythms Are Ignored   30

4. The 20-Minute Break:
   The Ultradian Healing Response   47

5. The Ultradian Toolbox   70

6. Maximizing Performance: Ultradians and the
   Worlds of Work, School, and Sports   90

7. Ultradians and Diet, Weight Control,
   and Addictions   121

8. The Ultradian Family   140

9. The Synchrony of Love:
   The Ultradian–Sex Connection   160

10. Many Paths, One Goal   177

Ultradian Healing Response Survey   183

Sources   190

Index   203

PROLOGUE

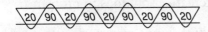

Have you ever found yourself

- feeling overwhelmingly fatigued in the middle of the day?
- spaced out or daydreaming during a meeting or conversation?
- making inexplicable errors over simple matters?
- suddenly unable to remember a familiar fact, name, or word?
- missing obvious social cues and saying the wrong things?
- right on the edge of anger, depression or tears without knowing why?

On the other hand, have you ever known times when you were

- feeling particularly healthy and in harmony with the universe?
- setting personal best records effortlessly?
- relating exceptionally well to family, friends, and others?
- unusually rested and energized after a short nap?
- performing surprisingly well in public and business meetings?

- quickly able to deal with problems you had been stuck on?
- easily coming up with creative solutions to problems?

You probably recognize both kinds of experiences, because we have all had them many times in our lives. Until recently, however, few people understood them for what they are—signs of natural peaks and troughs in a special kind of biological rhythm called ultradians (pronounced ul-TRAY-dians) that pulse through us every 90 to 120 minutes, creating a cycle of arousal, peak performance, stress, and rest in many of our key physical and psychological processes.

You may be familiar with the fact that our daily 24-hour circadian rhythms are important. These rhythms regulate our alternating periods of sleep and wakefulness every day. Ultradian rhythms, by contrast, are mind–body activities that have more than one cycle every twenty-four hours. While our circadian rhythms have only one cycle each day, ultradians may run a complete cycle every twelve, six, two, or less hours. It is the 90-to-120-minute ultradians, however, that are of particular interest in this book.

These Basic Rest–Activity Cycles modulate many of the key systems of mind and body—from our mental alertness, mood, and creativity to our energy, appetite, physical performance, memory, and sexual arousal. There is a rich rhythmic ultradian symphony of activity in our organs, glands, muscles, blood, hormones, and immune system that reaches down to our cells and genes. Our whole being heeds the call of these 90-to-120-minute rhythms over a dozen times a day, every day of our lives.

During the first hour or so of this rhythm, we swing upwards on a wave of heightened physical and mental alertness and energy, our skills, memory, and learning ability at their peak for dealing with the world around us. I call this the *Ultradian Peak Performance Period*.

Then, for the next fifteen to twenty minutes, we swing

down to a performance low at which we usually feel like taking a rest. In this phase, many of our systems of mind and body attempt to turn inward for a period of heightened healing and recharging for renewed endeavor. Our conscious mind apparently needs to take a break from its outer labors so that the deeper parts of the inner mind can catch up and pull everything together. I call this the *Ultradian Healing Response*.

Unfortunately, most of us—seduced by the world's demands and tightly organized schedules—habitually ignore and override the signs that our mind–body systems need to swing inward to the healing, revitalizing period for twenty vitally needed minutes every hour-and-a-half or so throughout the day. We try to avoid our normal 20-minute break that nature is calling for because we regard it as an inconvenience or a weakness.

When we chronically override this need for days, months, or even years on end, we interrupt the mind–body's natural ultradian rhythms of rejuvenation. This sets the stage for fatigue, stress, and psychosomatic problems throughout many systems of mind and body. Physically, this neglect can lead to stress-related problems of the body such as hypertension, ulcers, high blood pressure, and proneness to disease, along with the common everyday backache, headache, and other muscle pains. Psychologically, it can set off feelings of depression or incompetence, a lack of self-esteem, mood swings, and problems in relating well to others in love, work, and play. This is what I call the *Ultradian Stress Syndrome*.

This book is about how to recognize the telltale signs of ultradian stress in our lives and convert it to an Ultradian Healing Response. As you will see, by becoming aware of the natural rhythms of mind and body operating within us and properly utilizing the Ultradian Healing Response, we can significantly relieve the accumulated systems of stress, enhance our daily performance, and greatly improve our relationships and general enjoyment of life. Who would have thought that a mere 20-minute break several times a day could do so much?

EXPLORING AT THE EDGE OF SCIENCE

This book explores the leading edge of science. Although still controversial among scientists, the ideas and hypotheses herein are consistent with our most sophisticated understanding of human genetics, immunology, chronobiology (the biology of time), and other leading sciences. Often in these pages, our exploration of the Ultradian Healing Response will take us beyond the currently recognized and accepted truths. The purpose of this journey to the frontiers of mind–body science is to bring back something we can use to improve our lives, health, and well-being.

What is most profound about our developing understanding of ultradian rhythms is that they suggest a new approach to the classical mind–body problem—the scientific dilemma of how the mind and body communicate. How does something as solid and material as flesh and bone interact with something as gossamer as consciousness and spirit? How are the health and ills of mind and body related?

Until recently, we knew of no clear bridge between mind and body. Now our knowledge of ultradian rhythms suggests a new idea: Information is the new concept of our age that can bridge mind and matter. We now know that information in the form of messenger molecules expressed throughout our brain and body can modulate our mind, memory, and emotions as well as the physiological processes of every living cell of the body. In fact, we are now learning that many of the master messenger molecules that regulate mind and body are typically released in ultradian rhythms every few hours or so throughout the day.

Many researchers are now exploring the view that the healing traditions of many cultures—medicine man, shaman, faith healer, and hynotherapist—all tap into our natural Ultradian Healing Response without realizing it.

In the pages that follow, we will explore a trail of new ideas, never before presented to the general reader. Many of the findings come from research now being conducted at academic centers of genetic, behavioral, and biological science. Some of them come from military and government studies exploring the foundations and limits of human performance in critical areas of security. Many studies come from the research on human factors engineering, industrial psychology, and occupational therapy. Others are based on my own clinical observations over three decades of counseling people and those of hundreds of psychiatrists, psychologists, and therapists from around the world who are applying the principles of the Ultradian Healing Response to their work.

Many of the ideas in these pages could not have been known even a few years ago. They are entirely new to most practicing doctors as well as to many academic biologists and psychologists. Key aspects of this material are so new that they are being published in the scientific literature as I am preparing this manuscript. The professional reader will find an extensive list of documenting references presented in the chapter notes at the back of the book.

The purpose of this book is to introduce you to the healing art of the Ultradian Healing Response as a practical approach to enhance your own health and well-being. In chapters 1 and 2, I will explain how I discovered the Ultradian Healing Response and what science now knows about our natural mind–body rhythms. In chapters 3 through 5, I will describe how you can either succumb to the Ultradian Stress Syndrome, psychosomatic problems, and addictions or learn how to use the Ultradian Healing Response to cope with the increasing demands of modern life. Chapters 6 and 7 outline how you can use the Ultradian Healing Response in diet control and in maximizing performance in work and athletic training. Chapters 8 and 9 explore how we can learn to use our natural mind–body rhythms to get in social synchrony with each other to enhance familial harmony and sexuality. In the conclusion, we summarize some of the profound implications of understanding our mind–body rhythms for a broader

XII   *The 20-Minute Break*

theory of consciousness and meaning in the human condition.

Each time we take a quantum leap in extending the frontiers of human knowledge, we fundamentally change the ways in which we see ourselves, lead our lives, conduct our relationships—even the ways in which we structure our societies. Over 100 years ago, Dr. Sigmund Freud and his colleagues were groping to elucidate the workings of the unconscious mind. At that time, the idea of a hidden emotional life roiling within each of us seemed only one step removed from the world of magic and demons. Today, these topics are taught in high school, explored by millions of people in psychotherapy, and known by hundreds of millions through popular books, magazines, and television talk shows. Having spent the last century systematically elaborating theories of the unconscious, we can now intervene effectively in the hidden workings of the unconscious to improve psychological and social functioning.

Similarly, 50 years ago we had only the dimmest notions of the profound effects of exercise, diet, and stress on our health, longevity, and well-being; we knew almost nothing of their effects on the mind and body. In those days, one could scarcely have imagined that millions of Americans would run several miles a day, that health clubs would sprout like mushrooms throughout shopping malls, and that terms such as *low-impact aerobics* would become ordinary cocktail-party talk. Recent advances in nutrition have changed the way most of us eat, and our knowledge of stress has changed the way many of us work and play. Each advance in information in some way has changed our lives.

In the same manner, our understanding of ultradian rhythms can optimize those periods throughout the day when we are at our best, mentally and physically. The ultradian perspective opens a new window on mind–body relationships and offers us many new tools to help us attain higher levels of health, performance, and personal growth.

AN IMPORTANT NOTE

When people first hear about ultradian rhythms and the Ultradian Healing Response, they often ask, "Are these related to birthday-based biorhythms?" Absolutely not!

It is extremely unfortunate that the term *biorhythm* has become misunderstood through the popularization of the idea that we all have a 23-day physical cycle, a 28-day emotional cycle, and a 33-day intellectual cycle that are tied to our birth dates in some astrological manner. Birthday-based biorhythms are a myth. The books that give detailed instructions for charting one's birthday-based biorhythms are without any scientific foundation whatsoever. This popular but false theory is based on the work of a 19th-century Viennese doctor, Wilhelm Fleiss, and a few others who claimed that one's biorhythms begin at birth and persist rigidly unchanged throughout life. There is no scientific evidence that we can chart and predict when we will have good or bad days. More than a score of studies have shown no correlation between such fanciful birthday-based biorhythms and mood, accidents, illness, or daily intellectual, emotional, and physical performance.

One of the best summaries of the false science of birthday-based biorhythms comes from an anthology of research papers edited by Dr. Frederick M. Brown, a professor at Pennsylvania State University and noted expert in ultradian rhythms:

> A major problem with the pseudoscience of biorhythms, aside from its lack of congruence with any known naturally occurring cyclic phenomena, is the confusion that it engenders in the understanding and acceptance of bona-fide rhythmic functions that indeed have been demonstrated repeatedly by careful empirical clinical and laboratory experimentation.

Dr. Brown also notes that recent popular books resurrecting this mythology have worked "to the public's detriment in understanding actual biological and psychological rhythms."

In contrast, our current understanding of ultradian rhythms is based on hundreds of scientific studies, conducted in academic, medical, military, and industrial laboratories throughout the world. We know that our 90-to-120-minute ultradian rhythms affect a wide range of mind–body systems that modulate our lives, health, and performance in many subtle but significant ways. These ultradian changes have been established repeatedly by hundreds of biological and behavioral studies, many of which will be referred to in this book.

It is also important to understand that the Ultradian Healing Response is not related to such popular fads as auto-suggestion, self-programming, or affirmations. These methods of mind control presume to tell our inner nature what to do and how to be. But who among us is really wiser than nature? The Ultradian Healing Response, by contrast, teaches us to be sensitive to nature's own mind–body messages as they are expressed through our bodily responses, feelings, moods, and thoughts. As we learn to receive nature's signals with increasing understanding, we can create a more meaningful relationship to ourselves and others. As you read this book, we hope that you will join this ultradian odyssey, not just as a passive observer, but as an active participant. Learning to become aware of your ultradian rhythms and to use the Ultradian Healing Response is informative; it is no less important in life than eating well and exercising regularly to optimize your health.

In the interest of furthering research on the Ultradian Healing Response, a personal questionnaire is included at the end of this book. By filling it out and telling us of your own experiences, observations, and results, you will become a collaborator in our unfolding ultradian understanding. So please join us in the pages ahead in the shared hope that by living in ultradian awareness, all of us can dramatically change not just how we live, but how well.

1

ON THE TRAIL
OF A SCIENTIFIC
MYSTERY

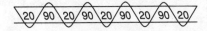

The discovery of the Ultradian Healing Response is composed of two stories—one psychological and the other in the realm of chronobiology, the biology of time. As with many puzzles of science, the whole picture does not emerge at once.

The trail of the ultradian mystery began with my experiences as a student of the late Milton H. Erickson, M.D., an eminent American psychiatrist. Between 1930 and 1980, he was renowned as one of the world's leading medical hypnotherapists and was the founder of The American Society of Clinical Hypnosis. Erickson is now regarded as one of the most influential thinkers in the history of recent psychotherapy.

As a therapist, Erickson possessed an uncanny grasp of people's deepest problems, strengths, and needs. Again and again, he cured those whom no one else had been able to heal. He somehow helped his patients become unusually receptive to their own patterns of personal growth. Under his care, they seemed uncommonly capable of opening doors to their inner mind with its hidden memories and its unique resources for healing.

Erickson's admirers praised his consummate skill in facilitating therapeutic hypnosis and the skill with which he resolved his patients' most deep-seated problems. His critics branded him a manipulative genius, an expert in subtly changing the human mind. *Time* magazine once called him "the Sorcerer of Phoenix." Yet all agreed that he was a remarkable virtuoso of the human psyche. By 1972, however, an elderly man overcome by polio and a number of physical handicaps, the world seemed to have forgotten him.

THE SORCERER'S APPRENTICE

A few years earlier, I had obtained my Ph.D. from Temple University in Philadelphia as a clinical psychologist and was starting my own practice. What I knew of Dr. Erickson intrigued me, so I sent him a copy of my first book, *Dreams and the Growth of Personality,* and requested an appointment. I didn't realize at the time that I was on my way to becoming his apprentice, but that is exactly what happened. For the next eight years—the final years of his life—I spent a week each month in his Phoenix home, recording sessions with patients, first as an eager student, then as a professional colleague, and finally as a research collaborator.

One of the most notable things about Dr. Erickson was that, while most therapists saw patients for fifty-minute sessions, he preferred to meet for ninety minutes or longer. In over a half-century of treating patients, Erickson had noticed that people quite naturally drift into distinct receptive states of mind in which they are more open to suggestions for therapy and healing. Working with patients for at least an hour-and-a-half, he found they were almost certain to enter this receptive state on their own. Erickson's sessions with patients seemed to be very subtle and indirect forms of hypnotherapeutic encounter wherein nature became an equal partner in ways that I could not understand at that time.

It soon became apparent to me that Dr. Erickson was not a genius of manipulation, as many believed, but rather a genius of observation. Behind his grandfatherly, sociable demeanor, Erickson watched his patients like a hawk, monitoring the tiniest changes in their physical and emotional states. He observed their pulse rates at spots on their face, neck, arms, and legs, where they were barely discernible. He watched the pupils of their eyes widen when important topics were discussed. During these lengthy sessions he noted that, for no apparent reason, the patient's head might start to nod rhythmically and the eyelids blink slowly, then close over farawaylooking eyes. The patient's body might go perfectly still, with fingers, hands, arms, or legs apparently frozen in an awkward position. Sometimes there was a beatific smile on the person's face—or, more often, the features were passive and slack, what Erickson described as "ironed out." During teaching sessions with me he often pointed out patients' rapidly quivering eyelids, furrowed brows, trembling lips and chin, and tears—the outward signs that these people were intensely groping with private inner dramas.

Erickson recognized that these subtle clues were important mind–body signals indicating that something of profound significance was being touched, even when people weren't consciously aware of it. It seemed to me that the secret of the famous Erickson magic lay in a phenomenally keen recognition of these signals that an emotional problem was coming to the surface.

Dr. Erickson always took advantage of this natural ebb and flow of consciousness that seemed to open and close like windows throughout his therapeutic sessions. Only after he observed that a window was opening and the patient's physical and mental processes were quieting down would Erickson facilitate hypnotherapeutic trance.

Years of treating patients had taught Erickson that during these healing periods, which usually lasted between ten and twenty minutes, his clients were able to gain better access to their emotions, intuitions, and deepest thoughts. He would use these windows of inner access to help people learn to solve their own problems in their own way. It was during these periods that Erickson did his most effective work helping his patients to achieve insights and behavioral changes that apparently were much harder for them at other times.

The Common Everyday Trance

Erickson called these natural periods of relaxation and healing *common everyday trances,* because they appeared to be a normal, spontaneous feature in daily life as well as in the consulting room. All of us have such moments during the course of the day, when we are in some in-between state of consciousness, neither fully awake nor quite asleep. The executive losing focus in a lengthy meeting, the housewife staring vacantly over a cup of coffee in midmorning, the student with a faraway look in his eyes during a lecture, the driver who blinks in mild surprise as he suddenly reaches his destination without any memory of the last twenty minutes—all are exhibiting the common everyday trance.

Although common, these brief periods of inner focus are clearly special. During these quiet moments we become more introspective. Our dreams, fantasies, and reveries—the raw material of growth in everyday life as well as in psychotherapy—become unusually vivid, as the window between our conscious and unconscious opens a bit. In these moments we edge closest to our inner mind and are more able to communicate with our inner selves. Because the inner mind is the source of our deepest knowing, people may be at their creative best during these meditative moments, experiencing insights, fantasy, and intuitive leaps. This window also allows us to remember much that could be of value in our lives but that remains out of reach at other times.

Erickson felt that it was important for young hypnotherapists to train themselves to observe these natural variations in human consciousness in normal life. And so, inspired by his therapeutic successes and hoping to use them in my own work, I began to compile lists of the subtle mental and behavioral signs my mentor had been using to identify the common everyday trance. Over the years, to improve my powers of observation, I watched people very carefully in normal daily living, waiting in a checkout line or sitting on an airplane, as well as in the consulting room. What I observed was that many signs of the common everyday trance were manifest in bewilderingly varied patterns in different people. Even the same person would evidence different patterns on different occasions. Some of these patterns included:

- facial features looking relaxed, calm, or blank
- staring vacantly, unfocused, into space
- yawning, or taking deep breaths or involuntary sighs
- slower reflexes, even clumsiness
- needing to stretch or get up and move around
- a growling stomach, hunger pangs, hiccups, or burps
- needing to use the restroom
- absent-minded jiggling of body parts
- lower, deeper voice quality
- absent-minded doodling
- lapses of hearing or tuning out of the outside world
- sleepiness and daydreaming

As I learned to recognize these natural periods of healing rest and receptivity, it became clearer that many of Erickson's so-called miracle cures were due to his exquisite sensitivity to these spontaneous shifts among many levels of consciousness when they took place in his patients. The longer I observed Erickson's work, the more I became convinced that his skillful use of these natural periods of the common everyday trance was an important key to the mystery of his therapeutic success. To Erickson, these moments were keys to the healing and transformation his clients experienced; they were central to his renowned therapeutic success.

We gradually realized that the secret of transformation from illness to health and higher levels of well-being lay in recognizing and facilitating a person's own mind–body resources during these brief natural windows of inner focus as they arose periodically throughout the day. We felt these special periods could be important for everyone, not just people in therapy. Because the unconscious is the source of creativity, emotion, and intuition, we believed that these windows of unconscious access could be used to encourage people's psychological growth and to help them find solutions to vexing personal problems.

But, as with many scientific developments, our new insight raised as many questions as it answered. Term it the common everyday trance, hypnosis, relaxation, meditation, daydreaming, or whatever—just what was going on during these special periods? Why did they occur? Had anyone else noticed them? How might they be used in other ways? Erickson didn't know, nor did anyone else.

To me, it seemed this mystery had reached an impasse. I never dreamed that findings from many diverse scientific disciplines would soon converge to answer the questions Erickson's work raised.

AN ULTRADIAN BY ANY OTHER NAME

The challenge to understand the mechanisms of Erickson's successful healing gripped me like a detective story. The next few years became a personal odyssey as I searched for other earlier discoverers of these ideas. As my reading progressed, it became clear that at least a century earlier many explorers of the human psyche had also observed and studied some of the characteristics and potential of the common everyday trance.

For example, in much of the work of the founders of depth psychology—French neurologist Jean-Martin Charcot, hypnosis pioneer Pierre Janet, Sigmund Freud, and the famed Swiss psychiatrist Carl Jung—I found clues that they understood something about our natural rhythms of consciousness and healing. Unfortunately, the biology of their time was not sufficiently advanced to detect subtle rhythms of mind and body that would have further illuminated their researches. They did not have access to the wealth of knowledge and technology we now have, including electrodes and EEG machines to read brain waves. They did, however, detect something important: subtle alterations of consciousness in everyday life that were related to health and well-being.

The first to notice something about the periodic nature of stress and healing was Charcot, a professor of neurology and psychiatry around 1850. Charcot believed that people periodically experience a state of consciousness somewhere between sleeping and waking, which he called hypnoid. He believed that this state was something like hypnosis but could appear spontaneously during daily life.

Charcot did not know why this hypnoid state appeared, but he hypothesized that it was much like the experience of being caught up in a dream at night. At such times, he believed, any strong emotional stimulus could become imprinted on the mind in an unhealthy or neurotic fashion. Particularly when we cannot rest, we become prone to highly charged emotional states, anxiety, irritability, and depression. Limited by the science of his day, however, Charcot searched in vain to find a biological basis for the hypnoid state.

The next to be puzzled by this phenomenon was Pierre Janet, one of Charcot's students, who also noticed that people experienced periodic fluctuations in mental energy at various times of the day. He termed these fluctuations *abaissement du niveau mental*—a lowering of mental energy. At such times most people feel tired and are not able to think or work at their best. If our stress is compounded by a traumatic or strong emotional event during these *abaissement* periods, the mind lacks its usual ability to make sense of the event and fit it properly into a meaningful, secure whole. At these times, we tend to be emotionally vulnerable and easily overwhelmed; we can register life experiences but cannot properly digest them. If we are severely criticized, for example, we may feel badly but are relatively helpless to do anything about the criticism because our defenses are down. The stressful experience remains within us unassimilated—in effect, jamming the gears of the mind.

Janet hypothesized that such unassimilated experiences could eventually become the seeds of obsessive thought patterns, phobias, or psychological and psychosomatic illness— problems that he believed were the result of the mind–body's continuing, frustrated effort to make sense of the original disturbing experience. Although the science of his day could not find it, Janet believed there was an underlying physiological source of these *abaissements,* something linked to stress and exhaustion. One medical historian of his era summarized Janet's view as follows:

> Janet . . . seems to have believed that the day would come when [these physiological forces] could be measured. He considered that these forces were, to a great extent, connected with the condition of the brain and organs. . . . These forces can obviously be reconstituted in some way. . . . One of the main sources of this reconstitution is sleep. . . . The same could be said about the various techniques of rest and relaxation, *the distribution of pauses throughout the day,* of rest days during the month, and of vacations during the year. . . [italics added].

In his understanding of the reconstitutive powers of "pauses throughout the day," I believe Janet was anticipating the value of the therapeutic potential of the natural mind–body periods of rejuvenation that I call the Ultradian Healing Response.

Many of Janet's ideas were adopted a generation later by Freud, who believed that the hypnoid state was related to abnormal states of consciousness as well as ordinary everyday "absences of mind." Freud wrote:

> A great variety of states lead to "absence of mind." . . . An investigator who is deep in a problem is also no doubt anesthetic to a certain degree, and he has large groups of sensations of which he forms no conscious perception; and the same is true of anyone who is using his creative imagination actively.

Like Freud, Jung also described a spontaneous shift of consciousness that he believed was associated with psychological problems as well as with creative work in healthy individuals. Jung's description of the rhythmic or wavelike character of these changes remained our clearest formulation for almost fifty years until our scientific discovery of mind–body rhythms:

> Certain experimental investigations seem to indicate that its intensity or activity curve has a wavelike character, with a "wave-length" of hours, days, or weeks.

Most striking in the work of these four pioneers was the progression of thinking about the nature and purpose of the common everyday trance. While for Charcot, the hypnoid state was a source of psychopathology, Janet expanded the concept to recognize that such moments of lowered energy during the day were a loss of the conscious mind's ability to synthesize information because the mind–body needs to rest. Freud then took Janet's idea one step further, proposing that the border states between consciousness and sleep are actually gateways to creativity as well as psychopathology, depending on how one relates to this alternation of consciousness. Finally, Jung took the last step: he saw in these border states the seeds for sustained higher states of consciousness, spiritual transformation, and breakthrough creative ideas. My research on these four pioneers had brought me back full circle to my work with Erickson and the special windows of healing that he called the common everyday trance.

THE BIOLOGY OF TIME

The next step in understanding the ultradian puzzle involves the biology of time. Since the 1950s, scientists in biomedical and military laboratories across the country had detected many subtle inner rhythms of the body and brain. Beginning with research on sleep and dreams, scientists discovered a vast number of interrelated rhythms—many of which appeared in widely varying patterns every 90 to 120 minutes or so. They called these ultradian rhythms, since they took place many times a day.

These hidden rhythms were so interesting that the government began spending millions of dollars to investigate them. These government researchers were particularly interested in learning more about human performance failure: plane accidents caused by pilot error when there was no mechanical malfunction; mistakes when radar operators failed to react to a crisis as appropriately or as quickly as they had been trained to do; experiences of moodiness, irritability, poor judgment, and even mysterious psychosomatic illness by key personnel in jobs that required constant vigilance over long periods of time.

Ultradian researchers revealed that all these situations had a common factor, which we might call endurance stress. They found that people experienced 90-to-120-minute ultradian rhythms of activity and rest throughout the day. These consisted of a peak of heightened alertness and performance, followed by a trough of fatigue when most people felt like taking a break. These ultradian rhythms affected performance across an extremely wide range of mental and physical tasks: cognition, attention, concentration, learning, short-term memory, creativity, eye-hand coordination, athletic ability, reflexes, and energy level.

As more scientific data emerged during the 1970s and 1980s, an incredibly diverse array of ultradian rhythms became evident behind the mask of so-called normal everyday activity. There appeared to be regular rhythms of activity and rest every 90 to 120 minutes or so among many systems of mind and body. It seemed that people had a very real need to take a break every hour and a half or so to rejuvenate themselves in order to perform at their peak again. This apparent need wasn't just laziness or submitting to union demands; people felt they needed to stop work, relax, guzzle coffee or cola, and eat snacks, in their struggle to whip their minds back into focus.

This ultradian research, although little known, is scientifically very significant. Unfortunately, as often happens in science, discoveries in one area remain unknown in another. Because of this, the valuable information compiled by ultradian biologists remained generally unrecognized by mental health professionals until a number of years later.

SOLVING THE MYSTERY

As I followed the emerging scientific data, something about these ultradian rhythms with their peaks and troughs seemed tantalizingly familiar. One day, when I was brooding over the details of the activity and rest phase of each rhythm, I suddenly realized what it was: the behaviors that we experience during the rest phase of ultradian rhythms were the same as the common everyday trance that Milton Erickson and I had identified and written about half a dozen years before! This astonishing parallel between biology and psychology suggested an important relationship between the ultradian rhythms of the body and those of the mind.

How could this be a simple coincidence? The parallels between the ultradian rhythms of the mind and body were so clear! The troughs of our ultradian body rhythms and the windows into our unconscious minds both occur spontaneously, every hour-and-a-half or so. Both involve a 20-minute period of apparent decline in alertness and focus. And both are manifestations of the need we all feel every hour-and-a-half or two to take a break, to get away from our normal working activity. Studying the graphs and charts of these rhythms (see Figure 1) suggested that the common everyday trance occurs in the 15-to-20-minute transition time between the low end of one 90-to-120-minute activity–rest ultradian period and the beginning of the next.

When I showed the 78-year-old Erickson, in the last year of his life, this similarity between the rest-phase behaviors of ultradian rhythms and the common everyday trance, he was

THE ULTRADIAN PERFORMANCE RHYTHM

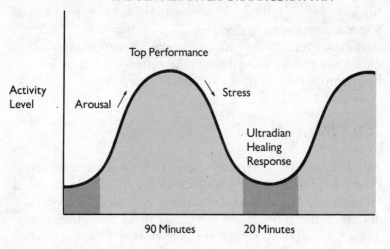

FIGURE 1. *The ultradian performance rhythm is a widely varying pattern alternating between 90 and 120 minutes of activity with 20 minutes of rejuvenation. There are wide variations among people and situations in the timing of these rhythms. They shift easily to help us adapt to the changing demands and circumstances of the real world.*

intrigued with the possible connection. He admitted, however, to never having realized his hypnotherapeutic healing methods could be tapping into verifiable, measurable rhythms of the mind–body. He had always described his approach as naturalistic; he was more naturalistic than he had known.

THE ULTRADIAN HEALING RESPONSE

These insights became the starting point for an entirely new theory about stress, health, and healing. Excessive and chronic overactivity leads to stress and symptoms by distorting our normal ultradian/circadian rhythms of activity and rest. The 20-minute Ultradian Healing Response ameliorates the symptoms of stress by providing an opportunity for our natural mind–body rhythms to normalize themselves. In other words, the 20-minute trough of our basic rest–activity cycle is a natural period for physical and psychological rejuvenation and healing from the wear and tear of everyday life. This is why I call it the Ultradian Healing Response.

The implications of the Ultradian Healing Response are important for a wide range of everyday experiences.

- Ultradian rhythms signal fundamental patterns of communication between mind and body that coordinate many physiological and psychological processes a dozen times each day.

- At the peak of each ultradian rhythm, nature has given us a powerful, naturally occurring opportunity to work and feel better by recognizing and utilizing these periods during which we are at the optimum level for activity.

- Every 90 to 120 minutes, nature has given us a 20-minute window to allow our mind, body, and psyche to regain balance and health amid the constantly shifting changes and challenges of daily life. We can learn to heed this natural ultradian call for rejuvenation and recovery, transforming ourselves from stress to health, from inefficiency to productivity, and from weakness to strength.

This suggests the view that the Ultradian Healing Response also may be the hidden common factor in most holistic approaches to mind–body healing. From the relaxation response and meditation, to imagery, biofeedback, hypnosis, spiritual rituals, and even the "laying on of hands," all such approaches require that the patient take a break for about twenty minutes to maximize their healing.

In the next chapter, we will examine more about the nature of our ultradian rhythms and the profound effects they have on our mind and body systems.

2

THE MIND–BODY RHYTHMS OF SELF-REGULATION

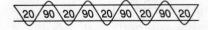

> *Not knowing that one has a time structure is like not knowing that one has a heart or lungs. In every aspect of our physiology and lives, it becomes clear that we are made of the order we call time.*
>
> DR. GAY GAER LUCE
> Report of U.S. Department of Health, Education, and Welfare

Science has long known that virtually every organism—from paramecium to pachyderm—is born, lives out its days, and dies influenced by a complex web of rhythms interwoven in time. Indeed, rhythm is the one constant of nature. Fruit flies and potted plants, sea slugs and nuclear physicists—all living things follow their own hourly, daily, and seasonal rhythms of activity and rest.

We are created as creatures of rhythm by our cosmic mother, the Earth, who generates a mandala of interlacing cycles. Her yearly pass around the sun, the shifts of her axis that bring the seasons, her daily rotation have a far greater influence on our lives and the life we share with her than we imagine.

Each day at the same time, honeybees in a garden gather

their nectar, following rhythms prescribed in their genes. Above them, the common starling forages for food, feeds its young, then forages again in fixed, clearly discernible six-minute rhythms. The hibernating bear, the migrating whale, and the spawning fish all observe daily, monthly, and seasonal rhythms of activity and rest. Ants and crayfish, rats and hamsters show clear daily patterns of sleep and activity, nesting and eating even when shielded from light in controlled laboratories.

For over two hundred years we have known that the leaves of plants open and close, lift and droop in rhythms of approximately twenty-four hours—even when they are isolated from the sunlight in deep caves. This surprised researchers because it meant that the source of plant rhythms lay within the plant itself rather than in the external rising and setting of the sun, as superficial observation would suggest. The internal source of plant rhythms was finally confirmed in 1985 when researchers at Rockefeller University discovered a genetic source of the rhythms. Sunlight can reset this genetic clock, however, speeding it up or slowing it down to keep pace with the changing seasons.

Although few of us realize it, humans also have genetic clocks that are influenced by the Earth's seasonal rhythms. Births, deaths, physical energy, and even mood have been proven to vary with the time of the year. Performance and alertness have been discovered to peak and decline on a monthly basis in both women and men. Our mental capacities, emotional state, blood chemistry, muscle strength, eye–hand coordination, and even resistance to disease vary in predictable rhythms throughout each day.

So pervasive and important are these rhythms that scientists have given them names. When biological rhythms rise and fall once each day, as do our sleeping and waking patterns, scientists call them *circadian* (*circa-dies,* "about a day"). When they take longer than a day, as does the monthly menstrual cycle, they are termed *infradian* (*infra-dies,* "below" or "longer than a day"). When these rhythms cycle many times throughout the day, as do hunger and sexual arousal, they are called *ultradian* (*ultra-dies,* "beyond" or many times per day).

Before we explore how our ultradian rhythms can have so deep and all-embracing an influence on performance, stress, and healing, we first need to appreciate the role played by the longer infradian and circadian cycles.

OUR SEASONAL RHYTHMS: THE INFRADIANS

The best-known individual infradian is the rhythmic waxing and waning of the menstrual cycle in women once every twenty-eight days or so. By now the dramatic influence of these monthly rhythms on mental as well as physical functioning is well documented. Typically, when estrogen levels reach their monthly peak just before ovulation and in the ten days before menstruation begins, women perform better on verbal and motor tasks but less well on spatial orientation tasks. As estrogen levels fall, the pattern reverses.

What few people realize is that men also respond to monthly rhythms. In a study that took place over sixteen years, Dr. Franz Halberg of the University of Minnesota Medical School discovered a clear 30-day rhythm in the levels of certain hormonal messenger molecules in the urine of his male subjects. This may explain the results of a study of rhythms carried out by Dr. Rex Herser at the University of Pennsylvania on a group of healthy male industrial workers. Almost all of the men were found to experience regular monthly rhythms that affected their mood changes, from energetic optimism to sullen depression. Other studies have found that violence, aggression, crime, and psychotic crises follow a fairly regular monthly pattern in males.

Another little-known infradian cycle is a psychological condition called seasonal affective disorder (SAD)—the "winter blues" or the "February blahs"—which affects one out of every ten people. During the winter in cold climates, when there is less sunlight, many people find their mental and physical energy levels reduced and tend toward depression, finding it difficult to cope with everyday tasks. Some researchers theorize this mind–body trough may have much in common with hibernation in bears and may be a genetic carry-over from a time when humans, too, spent the winters retreating in caves.

Science has also uncovered many other human mind–body rhythms that are also influenced by the Earth's four seasons. For example, twins are more likely to be born in May, June, and December; ulcers seem to occur most often in the first half of the year; diabetic problems become more common in winter; more people die of atherosclerotic hardening of the arteries in January; more suicides occur in May and September. There are probably other infradian rhythms that remain to be discovered. While science is still trying to figure out their causes and exact influence on us, we do know that they are undeniable forces that contribute to the nature of our being and consciousness.

OUR DAILY RHYTHMS—THE CIRCADIANS

Our knowledge of the relationship between our circadian and ultradian rhythms has progressed through three stages. Originally, it was thought that our circadian rhythm was simply a daily alternation between being awake and asleep. The second stage of our developing understanding began when researchers in the 1950s discovered that sleep was divided into 90-to-120-minute ultradian alternations of dreaming and deep sleep. Stage three began in the 1970s when researchers realized that we experience natural 90-to-120-minute ultradian alternations in our consciousness even when we are awake during the day. (See Figure 2.) It is now believed that our daily circadian rhythm is actually composed of a series of the more frequent 90-to-120-minute ultradian rhythms.

Many people notice regular shifts of energy and mood periodically throughout the day. There are wide variations

Stage One: A Daily Alternation of Being Awake and Asleep.

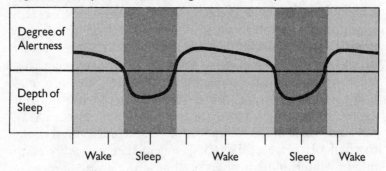

Stage Two: An Ultradian Rhythm of Dream (REM) Sleep (Aserinsky, Kleitman, 1953)

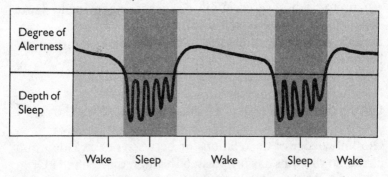

Stage Three: The New Model of The Ultradian Nature of Human Consciousness (Wever, 1985)

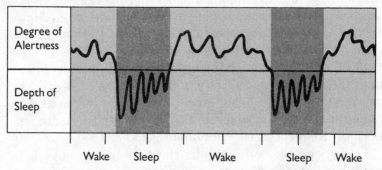

FIGURE 2. *Three stages in the evolution of the current model of the ultradian nature of consciousness. (Adapted from Wever, 1988.)*

among people in the timing of activity rhythms. Some people—colloquially called larks—perform best and are at their most alert in the morning, while others—called owls—perform best and are most alert in the evening. Studies indicate that a typical day carries many of us through the following circadian/ultradian patterns at the deepest levels.

Midnight

Preparation for a new day begins during the first hour or two of sleep, when cholesterol synthesis in the liver is at a peak. Although high levels of cholesterol can be dangerous, it is a vital substance that forms the basic building block for the daily production of a wide array of important hormones and other messenger molecules that affect everything from sex drive and moods to energy level and productivity.

2:00 A.M.

Within the first two hours of sleep, growth hormone is released to facilitate the building and repair of tissues throughout the body. As we sleep, the pineal gland in the brain releases a major hormone, melatonin, that modulates growth, sleep and dream patterns, the immune system, and the aging process.

3:00 to 4:00 A.M.

Most of our mind–body systems, including alertness and memory, along with the functioning of our organs and our core body temperature, reach their lowest levels around this time—whether we are awake or asleep. Consequently, this is the time when some of the worst human errors are committed by sluggish shift workers, pilots, taxi and truck drivers, and all others whose work schedule requires that they be up and functioning through the night. However, night owls and those with good circadian flexibility may perform adequately during this time.

5:00 A.M.

As we approach daylight our periods of dream sleep become longer and our dreams more sensible. Sometimes we awaken out of an early-morning dream with a new insight about an important issue facing us in the day ahead. Early-morning awakening often signals that our inner mind is intensely occupied with resolving important psychological issues.

6:00 to 9:00 A.M.

As our energy hormones reach their maximum, we awaken. Even the consistency of our blood is enriched to get ready for the day's activity. Within a few hours after awakening, we are ready for our first Ultradian Healing period.

10:00 A.M. to Noon

For larks, this is often the most productive part of the day. Memory and learning—in fact, most of our mind–body systems oriented toward work and performance—are approaching their maximum. Many creative workers find this to be the optimal time of the day for solving difficult problems and making important decisions.

Noon to 2:00 P.M.

Almost everyone experiences a postprandial (after-lunch) dip in performance. For many cultures, the early afternoon signals siesta time. Many creative people nap at this time and often awaken refreshed and full of new ideas. Winston Churchill, Prime Minister of England during World War II, probably said it best:

You must sleep some time between lunch and dinner, and no half-way measures. Take off your clothes and get into bed. That's what I always do. Don't think you will be doing less work because you sleep during the day. That's a foolish notion held by people who have no imagination. You will be able to accomplish more. You get two days in one—well, at least one and a half, I'm sure. When the war started, I *had* to sleep during the day because that was the only way I could cope with my responsibilities.

3:00 to 4:00 P.M.

Researchers have called this period the breaking point. After this point, the arc of our circadian consciousness, which has been on the ascendant, begins its downward curve. The entire mind–body is reorienting from outer-world performance toward sleep, our inner world of nurturing, healing, and restoration.

5:00 to 7:00 P.M.

This is the time when families reassemble for better or worse. Returning to a happy, supportive family can be a welcome and healing period. It is an optimal time for us to nurture ourselves and others. However, if we have ignored the ultradian call for restoration throughout the work day and return home overwhelmed by stress and fatigue, this period can be a time of misunderstandings, arguments, mental, and even physical, abuse.

8:00 to 10:00 P.M.

During this time the body prepares for sleep and rejuvenation at the deepest levels. There is a peak in cell division, for example, that can facilitate natural processes of growth and healing around 10:00 P.M.

OUR HOURLY RHYTHMS: THE ULTRADIANS

Technically, ultradian denotes rhythms that cycle many times a day—and that are measured in terms of hours, minutes, and even seconds. For instance, the heart beats out an ultradian rhythm some 86,000 times a day. Our breathing rises and falls about 22,000 times a day. Other readily observable rapid ultradian rhythms, which may occur several times a minute, include blinking and swallowing.

Approximately twelve to sixteen times every day, we experience the effects of many 90-to-120-minute ultradian rhythms that regulate activity and restoration throughout the mind and body. This ubiquitous rhythm of 90 to 120 minutes of activity and fifteen to twenty minutes of rest is considered so important that it has come to be called the *basic rest–activity cycle* (BRAC).

As mentioned above, scientists first discovered the basic rest–activity cycle through research on sleep and dreaming. In 1953, Eugene Aserinsky and Nathaniel Kleitman of the University of Chicago reported that rapid eye movements (REM) took place every ninety minutes or so throughout sleep. In these periods, our mind–body crackles with intense bursts of communication and activity. During REM sleep, more blood actually flows to the brain and the brain's pattern of electrical activity looks almost the same as it does when we are awake. Oxygen consumption and respiration, blood pressure, heart rate, and gastrointestinal activity all increase.

Further investigation revealed that it is during REM sleep that our dreams take place. Most adults apparently experience these dream rhythms associated with REM every 90 to 120 minutes throughout the night, whether or not they remember having dreamed when they wake up the next morning.

Research at the Boston University School of Medicine soon confirmed that these rhythmic mind–body changes are not limited to sleep but are simply most obvious at that time.

MIND–BODY ACTIVITIES
MODULATED BY ULTRADIAN RHYTHMS

Mind	Body
right-left brain dominance	left-right nasal dominance
attention	autonomic nervous system
concentration	gene-cell metabolism
learning	endocrine system
memory	immune system
sensations	breastfeeding
perceptions	hunger and sex
emotions	digestion
dreaming	work and sports
fantasy	stress response
imagination	psychosomatic responses
creativity	cellular metabolism
transpersonal sense	drug sensitivity

We can observe this same 90-to-120-minute basic rest–activity cycle operating in us twenty-four hours a day. It is responsible for the patterns of arousal, peak performance, stress, and recovery that we experience every few hours. Just as we average a 20-minute dream period every 90 to 120 minutes during sleep, we have a similar period while awake when we are more prone to fantasy, daydreams, inner focus, and rejuvenation.

In the past three decades, hundreds of research papers have demonstrated that an overwhelming number of the mind–body's systems run on this same 90-to-120-minute ultradian rhythm of peak activity followed by restorative troughs. In fact, research indicates that all our major mind–body systems of self-regulation—the autonomic nervous system (activity and rest), the endocrine system (hormones and messenger molecules), and the immune system (disease fighting)—have important 90-to-120-minute basic rest–activity cycles. BRAC discoverer Nathaniel Kleitman believes this rhythm is an essential, fundamental characteristic of the life process. The BRAC, he has written, "involves gastric hunger contractions and sexual excitement, processes concerned with self-preservation and preservation of the species"— which led to the designation *basic*.

When such fundamental human processes as learning and performance, digestion and bodily repair, and sex and personality all respond to the call of 90-to-120-minute rhythms—when even our muscles, glands, circulatory system, and organs resonate to it, and our very brain and psychological state keep time to it—these rhythms, or whatever causes them, must reflect pervasive patterns of communication between our mind and body. Yet how does this occur?

MESSAGES, MOLECULES, AND MIND–BODY COMMUNICATION

We now know that the answer to this basic question lies in the messenger molecules of the mind–body. All our major mind–body systems are orchestrated by messenger molecules that are released between mind and body in ultradian rhythms every 90 to 120 minutes throughout the day. Among the messenger molecules are sexual hormones, such as testosterone and estrogen; energy factors, such as glucose and insulin; and stress factors, like cortisol, adrenalin, and beta-endorphin, which modulate emotional states of arousal and relaxation. Many researchers now believe that these messenger molecules are the basic channels of communication between mind and body.

Because they carry signals throughout our mind–body, coordinating everything together into a whole, scientists also call these messenger molecules *informational substances*. These messengers tell us when we are hungry or full, stressed or relaxed, when we need to release energy and when to rest and revitalize ourselves. They regulate our energy level, pain threshold, sexual drive, thirst, alertness, anger or pleasure, and mental outlook, affecting all of our psychological and physical experiences. Informational substances (messenger molecules) run the show.

However, it is also important to understand that this periodic release of messenger molecules, while it regulates our mind–body activities, does not mean that we are controlled by our hormones. We know that our thoughts, attitudes, and emotions can influence the release and flow of these messenger molecules just as they can influence our thinking, feeling, and behavior. When something good happens to us, the mind–body responds by releasing the messenger molecules that enhance our feeling of excitement and pleasure. Likewise, when we face an unexpected reversal, our mind–body releases the messenger molecules that deepen our sense of sadness and disappointment.

The communication channel between mind and body flows both ways. Just as our bodies can communicate with our minds via messenger molecules, research suggests that mind communicates with body via the same route. Recently Candace Pert, former chief of brain biochemistry at the National Institute of Mental Health, described these messenger molecules as the biochemistry of emotions. Speaking of the messenger molecules and their receptors at the cellular level, she proposed that they make up a psychosomatic network that is the basis of mind–body communication.

THE ULTRADIAN SOURCE: THE MIND–GENE CONNECTION

Although messenger molecules are associated with the 90-to-120-minute basic rest–activity cycle throughout the mind and body, the source of this association has been approached only recently. New strides in unraveling the molecular biology of cells indicate that the messenger molecules of the mind–body's ultradian rhythms actually arise from the fundamental informational matrix of life itself—our genes.

Research on plants and animals ranging from yeast to trees and from snails to mice has found ultradian rhythms at the most basic cellular and genetic levels of all forms of life. The genetic basis of the 90-to-120-minute BRAC is evident in life's most fundamental process: cell division and growth. It has been found that once a cell is committed to division, it follows the BRAC timetable. A 20-minute period is required to build up an optimal concentration of cyclin, a messenger molecule that facilitates the process of cell division. The entire process of cell division then requires about 90 to 120 minutes to take place.

Recent research on this genetic source of our 90-to-120-minute ultradian rhythms also sheds new light on how mind–body communication can operate as a two-way process. It has been estimated that humans have about 100,000 genes. Most of these are self-regulating on purely physical and biological levels in specific tissues of the body and are not available for mind-gene communication. About 30,000 of our genes, however, are called housekeeping genes, because they are continually interacting with signals from the environment and apparently respond to the psychosocial world in which we live. It now appears that mind may be in constant communication with about one-third of our genes. We are only on the threshold of understanding this mind-gene connection; we need much more research to determine how it operates.

THE ULTRADIAN–PERFORMANCE CONNECTION

In the 20-minute rejuvenation phase of the basic rest–activity cycle, our mind–body catches up on much of the housekeeping necessary for our complex systems to continue functioning smoothly together. Messenger molecules carry signals between mind and body to integrate many critical processes of healing and growth. Deep within our bones, new blood cells form, millions every second, to carry oxygen and nutrients to every cell. The trillions of cells that make up the body refill tiny sacs on their inner walls, called vesicles, where they store messenger molecules. These stores become depleted as instructions are carried to the brain, nervous system, and organs during the active phase. The body busily replenishes the energy stores in the pituitary and hypothalamus, the adrenal glands, and the endocrine system, so that we can once again perform at our best during the active phase of our basic rhythms of activity, restoration, and healing.

This suggests that the twenty-minute rejuvenation phase of the basic rest–activity cycle is important for the optimal performance of all of our major systems of self-regulation. The rejuvenation phase of the 90-to-120-minute ultradian rhythm provides a much-needed break from the psychological wear-and-tear of the world's never-ceasing demands, allowing us to catch up with unfinished mind–body business. Our mind shifts closer to an inner focus and begins to reorganize itself to accommodate our past experiences and synthesize new levels of meaning and understanding from them, while our unconscious attempts to pull together and make sense of all that is happening around us.

The most significant impact of the ultradian activity and rest cycle on our everyday lives is its effect on our mental and physical capacities of performance, learning, and problem solving. This ultradian–performance connection has profound implications for everyone, from students in the classroom to executives making decisions in the board room.

Among the key factors affecting performance, creativity, and learning that have been found to wax and wane in the 90-to-120-minute BRAC pattern are:

Verbal and spatial skills. Researchers have found that performance on verbal and spatial tests alternates throughout the day in a predictable 90-to-100-minute rhythm, as we move

from one phase of the BRAC to another—the result of the ultradian shifts between the two complementary hemispheres
of the brain.

Physical activity. U.S. Army scientists monitored spontaneous physical activity in a group of college-age volunteers.
Left alone in a sparsely furnished, quiet room, each of the subjects changed position or moved around with an unmistakable
113-minute rhythm.

Eye-hand coordination and memory. Psychiatrists at Harvard and Cornell universities observed volunteers' skills while
they were playing video games. The volunteers showed clear
peaks every eighty-six minutes in eye–hand coordination
and every eighty-eight minutes in learning and short-term
memory.

Mental alertness. One group of university researchers
tested subjects on complex tasks requiring extreme mental
alertness. Again, task performance varied in 90-to-120-
minute ultradian rhythms.

Creativity. Subjects' response to psychological tests that
measure creativity, such as the Rorschach inkblot test, have
been found to vary roughly every ninety minutes.

The significance of this research is clear. If we can learn
to become aware of our ultradian rhythms, we can tap into the
valuable relationship with our natural cycles, to enhance our
health, our performance, our ability to control stress, every
function that reflects the mind–body's activity/rest cycle.

By learning to heed the signs that we are entering the active phase of the ultradian performance rhythm, we can enhance our overall performance by focusing on demanding
tasks while our energy and alertness are on the upswing. And
by learning to heed the signs that we are entering the 20-
minute rest-and-rejuvenation portion of the rhythm, we can

properly restore ourselves so that we are at our performance peak when our energy and alertness rise again.

In the next two chapters, you will see how to identify your personal ultradian rhythms, how to avoid falling into the Ultradian Stress Syndrome, and how to utilize the Ultradian Healing Response.

3

STRESSING OUT:

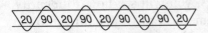

When Ultradian Rhythms Are Ignored

Because the clocks and calendars of social activity are designed for economic efficiency or convenience, an individual may have to learn to detect his own cycles, and become aware of scheduling to protect his health.

DR. GAY GAER LUCE
National Institute of Mental Health

Once upon a time, when our ancestors lived in nature, predators, other dangers, and exigencies of the natural environment made it impossible to drop everything every ninety minutes to heed the call of our ultradian rhythms. So evolution made our ultradian rhythms flexible enough to help us adapt to changing environmental circumstance. If we needed to make an extra effort at a particular moment, our ultradian rhythms would flex to increase our mental awareness and physical strength to survive in any emergency—even during the 20-minute trough. For while we needed to take rejuvenating breaks, it wasn't necessary to do so precisely every ninety minutes. The human organism could adapt to waiting awhile, or even skipping a restorative period now and then, just so long as we did take healing breaks on a fairly regular basis when there were no real world emergencies.

For eons our ancestors lived in close contact with nature's rhythms, waking with the sun and sleeping at nightfall, resting throughout the day when they felt the need. The relatively leisurely pace of natural life ensured that, by and large, when our ultradian cues signaled, we responded.

This system worked well during 99 percent of human evolution, approximately 135 million years. But in the last ten thousand years or so—a mere blink on the evolutionary scale of human development—something shattered this natural balance.

Over the course of a few thousand years civilization shaped us to live not by our natural rhythms, but by societal ones. Culture and governments instituted work schedules that disrupted our natural need for ultradian restoration, demanding that we push, push, then push some more. Ringing phones and traffic jams, deadlines and overdrawn checking accounts lock us in chronic states of stress. As artificial lights extend our active hours, we take less time to sleep. We relax less as we surround ourselves with cities, creating a plethora of diversions that keep us highly stimulated until exhaustion overtakes us.

Soon, the rising cacophony of civilized life, loud with distractions and stress, drowned out the relatively soft ultradian voice within. Now the very flexibility that had profound survival value in nature became maladaptive. What nature had designed as an exception—our ability to override our ultradian cues to adapt to short-lived emergencies in the environment—became the rule. Gone were the naturally rhythmic moments of quiet reflection and rejuvenation when we had always done our inner housekeeping. In their place, human consciousness became crowded with stimulation, distraction, and demands for more and more outer-world performance. It became progressively easier, if not obligatory, to neglect and ignore the inner cues of our Ultradian Healing Response.

The less we, as a species, heeded our natural ultradian rhythms, the less we noticed them. Eventually, most of us completely lost touch with our natural need for the periods of physical rejuvenation and mental rebalancing that evolution spent a hundred million years building into our mind-body systems and our genes.

Yet our innate need for restoration did not simply go away. It began to resurface in maladaptive ways, in which many of the natural rhythms involved in mind-body communication become disrupted—desynchronized, in researcher's terms. The human animal was never designed to live with chronic high levels of stress hormones. We can run at fever pitch for awhile, but eventually we damage ourselves when stress becomes chronic. Stress depletes our energy and stores of messenger molecules throughout our entire body, leaving the body flooded with fatigue toxins that set the stage for numerous stress-related problems.

We begin the stress cycle when we ignore the first signals that we need a break. When we push ourselves by continuing to work, the body expects we must have an important reason, and so it helps us perform by pouring out extra stress messengers and postponing its maintenance needs. But as stress and fatigue build up over a period of time when we consistently fail to heed our mind–body's call for restorative periods of ultradian healing, we become subject to the Ultradian Stress Syndrome.

THE ULTRADIAN STRESS SYNDROME

The Ultradian Stress Syndrome is a constellation of mind–body symptoms that can disrupt our lives when we habitually ignore our ultradian cues for rest and rejuvenation. Ultradian stress can lead to problems with memory, learning, accidents, burn-out, and self-defeating attitudes that can impair optimum work performance, well-being, and personal relationships. These diverse symptoms are all linked to the same underlying cause: neglecting the natural call for rejuvenation, creating physical and psychological fatigue, which, if ignored and allowed to build up, leads to far more serious stress-related problems including heart disease, stroke, and a variety of such psychosomatic symptoms as headaches, back pains, high blood pressure, ulcers, asthma, skin conditions, depression, anxiety, insomnia, obesity and compulsive eating disorders, suppression of the immune system, and proneness to such opportunistic illnesses as the common cold, the flu, and infections of all sorts. Some experts believe that accumulated stress, by suppressing the immune system, can even be a factor in cancer and AIDS.

Fortunately, once you begin to listen to your body and start taking the restorative breaks you need, your mind–body's self-regulatory processes will go to work replenishing the vital messenger molecules and restoring an optimal balance of health and well being. When that happens, even long-term problems of ultradian stress may be resolved.

Do You Suffer from the Ultradian Stress Syndrome?

Understanding the signs and stages of ultradian stress is helpful only if that knowledge helps you avoid it. These ten questions can help you determine whether you may be suffering from the Ultradian Stress Syndrome:

1. Do you suffer from stress-related health problems such as backaches, tension headaches, stomach or digestive problems, skin problems, asthma or high blood pressure?
2. Do you experience waves of depression, loss of self-confidence, and worry during periods of emotional fatigue throughout the day?
3. Do you often have problems with forgetting names or words, or forgetting where you put things when you are overtired?
4. Do you experience transient emotional swings, irritability, impatience, fleeting bad moods, teariness, or even crying spells at certain times of the day?
5. Do you have an out-of-control eating problem? Do you tend to overeat in the late afternoon or early evening, or sugar-snack throughout the day?

6. Do you have addictive behaviors such as the excess use of alcohol, cigarettes, coffee, chocolate, cola drinks, or other potentially harmful substances to raise your mood or calm you down?

7. Do you exhibit nervous habit problems such as nail biting, tics, hair pulling, finger sucking?

8. Do you find your important relationships stressful and conflict-ridden? Do you often feel you miss social cues, and misunderstand people?

9. Are you commonly accident prone, bumping into things, knocking over things, or spilling drinks? Do you make many errors in fine detail work after an hour or two of successful concentration?

10. Do you regularly have trouble falling asleep, or wake up without feeling truly refreshed from a night's sleep?

If you have experienced any of these signs in yourself, you may well be showing the effects of the Ultradian Stress Syndrome. Overwhelmed by the demands of the world, you have overridden nature's call for your ultradian healing period—without even being aware of it, you have desynchronized these crucial rhythms of mind–body communication and deprived yourself of your natural patterns of healing.

THE FOUR STAGES OF ULTRADIAN STRESS

My clinical experience suggests that the Ultradian Stress Syndrome progresses in four stages. You will recognize aspects of each of these stages from your own personal experience. Even if you have felt them often, however, you probably have not recognized what they were trying to tell you.

Stage One: Take-a-Break Signals

The take-a-break signals are the first mind–body cues that you need to take time out for inner rejuvenation, to break the cycle of stress generated by your activities. Your body has substantially depleted its energy reserves and the many messenger molecules that maintain mind and body in smooth synchrony. When the first take-a-break signals are sent by the mind–body to tell you the 20-minute rest and restoration period of the ultradian rhythm is about to begin, there is still time to heed them before the ill effects of the Ultradian Stress Syndrome occur. You are probably active and engrossed in whatever task is at hand. You are feeling good, so you plunge on. And everything is well for a while.

Then the signal intensifies. You suddenly experience a need to stretch and yawn. Perhaps your stomach rumbles, or you feel the urge to stretch your legs or to go to the restroom. You may heave a sigh, make a simple, careless mistake, or find yourself rereading the same sentence several times. You feel like taking a break to move about, walk to the water cooler, nibble on a snack, or smoke. You get the urge to chat with a friend. You feel good but ready for a brief change of pace. If you look at the clock, you will see that it is probably about 90 to 120 minutes since you started to work.

You are receiving a gentle reminder, a clear signal that you need to take a break so that your mind–body can restore itself from the stress and fatigue of your work.

Take-a-Break Signals

- feeling a need to stretch, move about, or take a break
- yawning or sighing
- finding yourself hesitating and procrastinating, unable to continue working
- noticing your body getting tense, tight, and fatigued
- pangs of hunger

- awareness of a need to urinate
- feeling "spaced out"; your concentration is poor, your mind wanders
- feeling depressed or emotionally vulnerable
- being distracted by fantasies, perhaps sexual
- slight memory problems; forgetting words "on the tip of your tongue"
- making careless errors in spelling, typing, or counting
- sharp drop in performance and output

By heeding these calls for a restorative break, you can escape the grip of ultradian stress and fatigue, give yourself the opportunity to balance brain hemispheres and nervous system, clear accumulated waste products from your tissues, and replenish supplies of messenger molecules within all your cells. Psychologically, such periods of ultradian inner focus help pull together the events and emotions of your life into a meaningful whole. The Ultradian Healing Response lets your mind reorganize itself to make sense of your experiences, give order to what is happening around you, and create new levels of meaning and understanding.

If you do not give your mind this opportunity, unfinished events may float in your unconscious and could become the seeds of psychological distress, obsessive-compulsive thought patterns, phobias, and anxiety. The mind keeps spinning its wheels, trying to do its job without its full working capacity.

Suppose, however, like many of us, you remain obsessed with the task at hand and try to overwork. Suppose your inner taskmaster plays a stern role: "Look, the work you have to do is really important, stop goofing off, no time to rest!" Or perhaps you are not even consciously aware of the initial take-a-break signals. You shrug, stretch, shake your head as if to clear the cobwebs, and push yourself to resume work.

You have just ignored your first chance for a restorative break. The Ultradian Healing Response is now a road not taken. The healing moment passes, and the Ultradian Stress Syndrome begins.

Nothing feels different immediately, yet already something has changed. Deep within the folds of your brain, in a region called the limbic-hypothalamic system, a series of stress-messenger molecules has begun to carry emergency signals to every corner of mind and body. The signals will rapidly touch every organ system in your body to bring you to the second stage of the Ultradian Stress Syndrome.

Stage Two: High on Your Hormones

Nature rarely gives us something for nothing. Our natural mind—body rhythms evolved to be easily overridden by important social and environmental cues. Ultradians are flexible in helping us adapt to the demands of the real world, but that adaptability comes at a price. We pay for it with an excess of stress hormones.

Such stress messengers were designed as a powerful short-term solution to an immediate, life-threatening problem. When a predator stalked one of our primate ancestors, stress-messenger molecules flooded the circulation. They sharpened nervous-system reflexes and increased alertness; sped the heartbeat, brought more oxygen to muscles to prepare for exertion; liberated the body's stored fuel from its storage place in the liver; and readied the muscles for immediate fight-or-flight. Stress-messenger molecules prepared the body to squeeze out every last drop of performance in risky but short-lived situations.

But what was helpful then can be harmful now. Modern stresses do not usually involve short, life-or-death confrontations. Our stress is rarely life-threatening, but rather chronic with all the nagging irritations of an overbusy life. The ringing phone, the angry boss, the rush-hour traffic, concerns about unpaid bills—none is really a life-and-death emergency. But your body doesn't know that, so it does what it was evolved to do in the face of apparent emergencies: it pours out stress-messenger molecules.

With all these stress hormones flowing, particularly adrenaline, within a few minutes you get the energy surge we call a second wind. You plunge back into what you were doing with a renewed feeling of energy. You may even be proud to have shaken off your fatigue. You are enthused and alert, riding high on an energetic, creative, achieving rush. You are excited and intent, feeling good, your fatigue and pain masked by a whole pharmacopoeia of natural opiates, such as beta-endorphin, a messenger molecule that lets you feel good even when you are under stress.

In this case our language accurately mirrors our life experience, and we speak of a rush of energy. You are high on your hormones; without realizing it you are already experiencing the ill effects of the Ultradian Stress Syndrome. For a while you may feel great and believe that you are functioning at your best—and to some degree you are. At this point, you are in a self-induced high state, one that sometimes borders on behavioral intoxication and even addiction.

In this second stage, symptoms of the Ultradian Stress Syndrome include speeded-up, hyperactive, and manic behavior; overpressured and rushed interactions; irritability, impatience, and flashes of anger; and self-absorbed, narcissistic, selfish behavior.

In such states, we often don't know how or when to stop. We may feel we are on top of the world, but actually we are more like the drunk who does not realize how extreme his behavior has become. Other people can see we are acting inappropriately rushed, self-focused, and short-tempered, but we are blind to our symptoms.

Who hasn't recognized the hyperactivity of a workaholic: the distracted boss zooming by in a blur of intense activity, obliviously making insensitive demands, as assistants roll their eyes at one another in exasperation? The typical results of becoming high on your hormones are tension, hostility, bruised feelings, reduced trust, grudges, and resentments. When these signs of the Ultradian Stress Syndrome occur chronically, they can seriously impair our relationships with co-workers, friends, and family.

Many medical experts believe that when people become chronically enthralled with the rush of this hormonal high, they set in motion the basic process of addiction. The hard-driving behavior that leads people to get high on stress hormones now appears to be similar to the stress-induced feelings of fatigue and depression that lead people to take drugs. We may turn to drugs and other substances of abuse in a search for an even greater rush than our natural hormones can provide. By trying to extend their high in an effort to become more productive, some people turn to coffee, alcohol, cigarettes, or cocaine, as well as other prescription and nonprescription drugs. When used to chronic excess, these substances only magnify the Ultradian Stress Syndrome, however, and lead to a vicious cycle of ever-increasing needs for artificial stimulation. Addiction in our society may be in many ways a response to the overwhelming stresses that continually push us beyond our means—all because we override nature's soft, sweet signals and ignore our need for regular restorative ultradian breaks.

Stage Three: Malfunction Junction

By now, your body's systems need replenishment more than ever. The tiny storage sacs within many cells of your brain and body that hold crucial messenger molecules like adrenaline are now near empty. With such low reserves, all the cells in your body are crying out for some time to replenish and rebalance themselves. But you are not about to stop—you are addicted to a hormonal rush, and it feels too good to quit now. Drugged by the high levels of mind-altering stress messengers coursing in your blood, you remain oblivious to the increasing ultradian cues for rest that your body is giving you. Distracted, numbed by the bliss-inducing beta-endorphins in your brain, you will continue to override your need for a quiet period of recovery and restoration.

By ignoring this need, however, you have now put yourself squarely on a collision course with your mind–body's

imperatives: you are already on the downhill slope of the Ultradian Stress Syndrome. You have disrupted the naturally restorative 20-minute phase of the ultradian rhythm. You are
headed for a losing showdown with the Ultradian Stress Syndrome.

Having reached stage three by suppressing your need for
restoration, your brain, body, and nervous system are beginning to malfunction. The hormonal messenger molecules that
coordinate memory, perception, and performance are depleted. Without realizing it, you are falling into a state of stress
and failing functions. That is when malfunction junction lives
up to its name: the usually smoothly functioning mind–body
systems begin to make mistakes that can have serious social
and personal consequences. Stage three of the Ultradian Stress
Syndrome is all about mistakes: silly mistakes, judgment mistakes, and physical mistakes, both little and big.

When you are at this malfunction stage, it seems you just
can't do anything—read, write, think, or even speak—with
your usual skill. Your sensory-perceptual capacities of seeing,
hearing, and touch are dimming much more than you realize.
Your reaction time falls below par, making you prone to accidents in work or sports. Memory begins to fail in a most dis-
mal and embarrassing way. You grow irritated with yourself
and impatient with others. Nothing seems to be going right.
Documented psychological and mental malfunctions at this
stage include:

- accident proneness, clumsiness, spilling things, and
  bumping into things
- judgment errors and bad decisions made despite knowing better
- repeated errors in spelling, typing, and computing
- significant memory problems, including forgetting
  what one was saying or looking for
- slips of the tongue, including misspeaking, using
  wrong words

- missing important implications in business and failing to understand puns and jokes
- flashes of impatience and irritation
- interpersonal miscues and social gaffes

It was probably this state of ultradian stress that French psychiatrist Pierre Janet was talking about when he noted that several times throughout the day we lose our synthetic capacity—our ability to effectively make sense of reality and keep things running in an orderly way. Every one of us has, at one time or another, hit stage three by ignoring our natural ultradian cues for rest and recovery.

When you consistently go into malfunction junction day after day, you may condition yourself into a chronic feeling of incompetence, coming to see yourself as a failure. In the depths of ultradian stress, your emotional reserves and defenses are lowered, because you don't have the energy to maintain them. In such moments, we are all poorer judges of what is true and what isn't, and it is easy to believe the worst about ourselves. "Look at this mess I've made," you may think; shaking your head in disgust. "I'm really incompetent!" Such negative self-assessments can overwhelm us if we continue to push ourselves into the Ultradian Stress Syndrome day after day.

In this stage you are highly suggestible, close to your unconscious, and it is easy to see every glass as half empty. When you are in malfunction junction, you simply don't have the mental energy to see your way to a possible resolution of your problems. It seems as if you will not be able to solve whatever problem you are facing. When prolonged states of ultradian stress continue and our negative self-talk becomes chronic, we lose our self-esteem and fall into psychological depression.

Perhaps you can identify with one of my clients, a successful architect, who consistently drove herself to malfunction junction because of her busy, demanding job. She would spend a grueling day at work, then attend social functions where she was supposed to meet potential clients. Unfortunately, having driven herself into serious chronic stress by ignoring her needs for relaxation and healing periods during the day, her mind–body reserves were at a low ebb. In one therapy session, she lamented having been introduced to several of the top brass of an important and new client company at the end of a nonstop day only to be mortified a few moments later when she couldn't recall their names. "God, I'm dumb! Careless! Inattentive!" she told herself, noticing that her competitor seemed to have remembered everyone's name. Feeling even more incompetent, she then nagged herself, "I never remember names!" This, of course, only made her more anxious and further distracted her from remembering names in the future.

Indeed, in urban pressure cookers and high-pressure businesses everywhere, with their intense emphasis on conspicuous achievement, therapists and business consultants constantly observe this paradox. High performers—including executives, directors, writers, lawyers, doctors, and engineers—stellar achievers all, often have a poor self-image, utterly convinced they are failures. These people are precisely those who continually drive themselves into the malfunction-junction stage of the Ultradian Stress Syndrome. When, inevitably, they finally fumble a task because of their inattention to the mind–body's need for rest and recovery, they interpret it as proof that they are weak or lazy, unable to perform in a crunch. This may explain why many highly regarded professionals become dysfunctional, depressed, and even suicidal.

Stage Four: The Rebellious Body

Unfortunately, not all people come to their senses and quit at malfunction junction. Some continue to ignore their mind–body cues for rest and recovery and remain hopelessly overwhelmed by what they imagine are the world's demands on them. These unfortunate people enter the last, and most de-

structive, stage of the Ultradian Stress Syndrome: the rebellious body. Such individuals, who chronically override and
disrupt their ultradian rhythms by ignoring their natural
periodic needs for recovery even after experiencing the clear
signals of failing functions in stage three, set in motion the
basic process of psychosomatic illness.

When we repeatedly ignore our need for natural ultradian
healing, our mind–body cannot repair and replenish natural
wear and tear, so it simply deteriorates. This neglect packs a
huge cumulative wallop. As we continue working, ignoring
the ever-more ominous negative signs of increasing stress, we
may begin to experience a variety of serious symptoms and
ailments.

These symptoms are caused by the accumulated effects of
chronically high levels of stress-messenger molecules. Hans
Selye, the pioneering Canadian neurophysiologist who is considered the father of modern stress research, demonstrated
that when stress piles up beyond normal levels, it causes physical damage to mind and body. We now know that excess stress
hormones can kill brain cells dealing with memory and learning. Such psychosomatic illnesses as stomach ulcers, headaches, backaches, muscles aches, and disturbed heart function,
and such respiratory difficulties as bronchitis and asthma, are
all associated with excess chronic stress. Stress also suppresses
the immune system, making us vulnerable to a host of opportunistic infections like colds and flus, and may even impair our
ability to fight off life threatening illnesses such as cancer.

Only in the last few years have we understood the ultradian piece of the stress puzzle. A fundamental source of
chronic stress is the suppression of our natural need for ultradian rejuvenation about every hour and a half. One way the
Ultradian Stress Syndrome may lead to mind–body symptoms
is by the chronic disruption of our natural basic rest–activity
cycle. Dr. Stanley Friedman, of the Department of Psychiatry
at the Mount Sinai Hospital School of Medicine of the City
University of New York, proposed that the mysterious bridge
of psychosomatic illness between mind and body may relate to

such malfunction. This implies that ultradian rest and restoration could lead to the improvement or complete remission of stress-related psychosomatic problems.

Evidence is continuing to accumulate that all of our mind–body systems of self-regulation can be seriously impaired by continually overriding our ultradian rhythms and ignoring our need for periodic ultradian breaks. The fourth stage of the Ultradian Stress Syndrome creates serious dysfunctions in four distinct areas.

Sleep problems. People who chronically fall into stage four—and especially workers whose hours vary constantly, requiring them to sleep and wake at different times—grossly disrupt their circadian and ultradian rhythms. Shift workers especially have been shown to suffer from much higher rates of work error and illnesses such as hypertension, stomach problems, breathing disorders, menstrual difficulties, and mental disturbance. In a study of ship's engineers who were on call and could anticipate having their sleep interrupted, it was found that their brain waves, heart patterns, and ratings of how well they slept were significantly disturbed even when there were no alarms or calls. The authors concluded that the sleep disturbances "were due to the apprehension and uneasiness induced by the prospect of being awakened by an alarm."

These findings have many profound implications for professionals and service-oriented workers such as doctors, nurses, paramedics, police, firemen, businessmen, and messengers whose ever-present beepers control their lives. Being on call is stressful. Appropriate ultradian recovery periods when one is not on call are necessary for health and well-being.

Gastrointestinal disorders. Since the first report of 90-to-120-minute rhythms in gastric contractions of the stomach, much evidence has accumulated linking disturbances of this ultradian rhythm to emotional and psychosomatic conditions. Butterflies in the stomach are often the first mind–body signal that we are anxious, tense, and emotionally involved; this same upset stomach is an early warning sign that the Ultradian

Stress Syndrome may have begun. In fact, gastrointestinal problems are one of the problems most frequently cited by shift workers and people experiencing jet lag.

More recently, a variety of hormonal messenger molecules that are released in ultradian rhythms have been associated with eating disorders such as anorexia nervosa, bulimia, and obesity. It has been found, for example, that the ability of growth-hormone releasing hormone (GHRH) to actually release growth hormone varies markedly according to the time of day as well as the person's degree of hunger. Normal women respond differently than obese or anorexic women: their food intake has an appropriately inhibiting effect on the release of growth hormone by GHRH, but in obese or anorexic women it does not.

The ultradian relationships between fasting and the release of growth hormone have been documented recently for both males and females. Further studies are needed to determine the degree to which a regular eating pattern that coincides with our natural 90-to-120-minute gastric rhythm can normalize conditions such as digestive and eating disorders. Even without such studies, however, it is obvious that we can optimize our well-being by heeding our ultradian call for food at appropriate times in appropriate amounts throughout the day. Chapter 7 will detail how using the Ultradian Healing Response can help in weight control and better eating habits.

Heart problems. Prolonged ultradian stress can disrupt the heart, according to research at the University of Oklahoma and Walter Reed Army Institute of Research. Scientists report that "The stable ultradian rhythm in heart rate is at first wiped out by the stress [situation]." As stress continues, they found, the rhythm tries to reassert itself but does so more erratically, with much wider-than-normal swings, leading to heart problems.

Shortened life span. Neglecting our periodic need for ultradian rest and healing can create longer-lasting and more serious effects. When researchers at the University of Minnesota Medical School put a group of mice on a constantly varying cycle of light and dark designed to throw their internal circadian and ultradian rhythms into disarray, the animals' average life span dropped by 6 percent—the equivalent of a loss of four-and-a-half years for a person. Dr. Franz Halberg has suggested that people such as transcontinental pilots and flight attendants, whose work keeps their inner rhythms constantly scrambled, may actually age faster.

The evidence makes it clear: we ignore our ultradian mind–body cues at our own risk.

BREAKING THE SPIRAL OF THE ULTRADIAN STRESS SYNDROME

Now that we understand the problem of the Ultradian Stress Syndrome and its most familiar features, we can look toward a solution. Instead of ignoring the ultradian call we must learn to appreciate our inborn rhythms of activity and rest for what they actually are: nature's wonderful way of balancing the outer world's demands for performance with our inner world's need to take time out for restoration, healing, and self-creation. By heeding the first take-a-break signals, we can avoid the destructive aspects of the Ultradian Stress Syndrome.

The next chapter will show how to break the downward spiral of the Ultradian Stress Syndrome by working with and getting the most out of the natural Ultradian Healing Response.

4

THE 20-MINUTE BREAK:

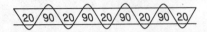

The Ultradian Healing Response

> *An important implication of studies of bio-rhythms and consciousness in Man is that, to raise the level of awareness, one should pay more attention to his body's natural variations and to matching them harmoniously with the environment.*
>
> ROGER BROUGHTON, M.D.

The Ultradian Healing Response is nature's own healing period, the mind–body's solution to the Ultradian Stress Syndrome. No matter how you have abused your ultradian rhythms in the past, or how much stress you have built up by overriding your inner calls for restoration, you have an opportunity to start making things better in the next 90 to 120 minutes. At this crossroad, you can heed nature's signals for healing and balance. You can learn to integrate your body and mind and begin to realize personal, creative, and healing potentials you never knew lay within you.

THE ULTRADIAN HEALING RESPONSE

Like the Ultradian Stress Syndrome, the Ultradian Healing Response is made up of four stages. However, these stages are not rigidly defined; they are offered here only as a guide. First

47

we will describe what happens in each stage and what that stage feels like. Throughout, we will offer ultradian tips, suggestions you can use to enhance your mind–body's healing. Then we will review some of the broader benefits of the Ultradian Healing Response—in performance, creativity, and consciousness.

Stage One: Recognition Signals

The Ultradian Healing Response begins with the same take-a-break signals that characterize the first stage of the Ultradian Stress Syndrome. What makes it healing rather than stressful is how you choose to respond. Instead of ignoring these early signs, you can recognize them for what they really are: your mind–body's first soft, sweet messages that you need to take a time-out and allow yourself to experience the restorative Ultradian Healing Response. It is important that you learn to interpret these indicators as a call to healing and rejuvenation rather than as a sign of weakness, inadequacy, or failure. You will find you experience them with a sense of comfort and well-being once you begin to understand them in this new light.

Following is a list of those signals, each a positive, vital, and natural mind–body message.

Recognition Signals

- wanting to stretch or loosen up your muscles
- yawning or sighing restfully and comfortably
- noticing your body becoming quiet, still, and relaxed
- feeling a desire for a snack and/or a mild urge to urinate
- experiencing happy memories and thoughts of good times
- feeling thankful, introspective, and confident your work is well done

- feeling comfort and emotional satisfaction
- having friendly fantasies and/or feelings of mild sexual arousal
- realizing your outer performance is slowing down while your access to inner healing is on the rise

By recognizing and responding to these signals as soon as they occur, you can enjoy them as invitations to calming, restorative rejuvenation. You don't have to do anything special—you will slip into the Ultradian Healing Response entirely without effort. Remember, this is a natural phenomenon that your mind–body will automatically access, unless you knowingly try to override it.

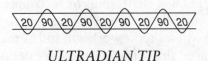

ULTRADIAN TIP

From now on, when you notice any of the first-stage take-a-break signals, greet them as the good news that you are about to enter the Ultradian Healing Response. Then relax comfortably as you proceed to slip into a natural state of mind–body healing that will take place without your conscious effort for the next twenty minutes or so.

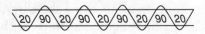

For most of us, the recognition stage requires a few minutes to make its presence felt, even if we are experienced in tuning in to our mind–body signals. Because the mind typically tries to screen out physical and psychological distractions when we are focused on a task, it usually takes our preoccupied conscious mind a few minutes to realize that these first subtle signals are calling.

In this initial recognition stage, a person with ultradian awareness will wonder, "Do these clues mean I am ready to take a break?" The answer is usually yes. In this stage, your unconscious mind will often float such a question into your waking consciousness like a trial balloon. Indeed, the very fact that such a question arises suggests that the conscious-unconscious balance in your brain has already shifted slightly toward your natural Ultradian Healing Response.

You can facilitate your entry into the Ultradian Healing Response by putting yourself, as best you can, in a quiet, undisturbed environment. The lack of outer stimulation will help enhance your mind–body's natural tendency to turn inward. Ideally, you might find a quiet place to lie down or close your office door and relax in a comfortable chair. Even a short walk in a park or some other relaxing location will help. The goal is to eliminate from your environment as much as possible any ringing phones, chattering conversations, all those insistent demands of the typical workplace.

The phone will wait; the work will still be there when you get back. You need this ultradian recovery period to soothe, heal, and rejuvenate now. Your mind–body wants this time to do its internal housekeeping to optimize the metabolic processes of rejuvenation and recovery, and to replenish messenger molecules and energy stores to their optimum levels.

Learning to believe your mind–body messages. Critics of self-nurturing therapies and ways of life often find fault with them for being narcissistic and self-centered. However, taking a conscious 20-minute break to allow the Ultradian Healing Response to repair mind–body stress is neither vain nor selfish. Such self-nurturance is nature's way; it is vital if we are to remain psychologically and physically fit. In fact, the very reason nature developed the basic rest–activity cycle was to make us slow down and take care of ourselves. This cultural prejudice against self-nurturance is one reason we characteristically override our ultradian call. It is a sad fact, but most of us have been programmed with negative attitudes toward taking time off and relaxing for a few minutes throughout the day. We tend to interpret the common signals that our body wants to enter the Ultradian Healing Response as signs of personal self-indulgence or weakness. The very terms *fatigue* and *rest* have pejorative connotations, suggesting an undesirable, depleted condition. So, think of it this way instead: when we heed our ultradian call we enter a state of rejuvenation, recovery, recuperation, recharging, restoration, or revitalization—all terms with positive connotations that carry a *re* prefix, indicating they are a part of a natural healing rhythm from the source of life itself encoded in our genes.

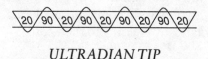

ULTRADIAN TIP

Do not berate yourself for being lazy or weak for needing rest. Reframe that negative self-evaluation into a positive, natural healing process. Engage in some supportive self-talk, such as: "Now I am entering my natural Ultradian Healing Response. I will let myself sit back, tune in, and let nature do whatever it needs to do to heal and revitalize on the deepest levels of my being. My mind—body has been helping me so much doing outer work in the last couple of hours, I will return the favor and let myself have the restoration and inner healing I now need."

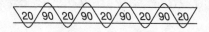

Another reason we override our ultradian calls so often is that we usually do not notice the changes they bring, even when they are occurring. Moving into the 20-minute rest-and-restoration phase puts us into a distinct state of not noticing as we turn inward. One ultradian research group, a combined project of the Veterans Administration and the University of California, was puzzled by people's constant failure to notice ultradian changes, even when they were rather significant.

"None of our subjects were aware of any rhythmic modulation in their mental functioning at the very moment they themselves were documenting their cycles in mental content. It is not obvious how so profound a modulation of experience might influence waking subjects without introspective recognition," researchers reported.

Because the signals of the Ultradian Healing Response are subtle enough to readily adapt to changing conditions around us, they are often drowned out by the more pressing clamor of the outer world. But as you pay attention to them more and more, you will become more adept at recognizing them and automatically yielding to their call.

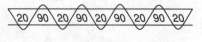

ULTRADIAN TIP

Some people require days, whereas others need a few weeks, to observe and attune themselves to their Ultradian Healing Response. We each move at our own pace, and there are no absolutes. The real guide is never the clock or the calendar, but your own feelings and experiences.

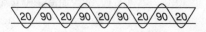

Stage Two: Accessing the Deeper Breath

If you act on the initial recognition signals and allow yourself to take time out for the Ultradian Healing Response, you will soon notice a shift in your breathing pattern. Spontaneously, naturally, involuntarily, you will find yourself taking a deeper breath or two, heaving a comfortable sigh or yawning, and noticing that the rhythmic rise and fall of your chest is smoothing out and quieting down. This is the signal that you are entering stage two of the Ultradian Healing Response: accessing the deeper breath.

This change in breath means that your sympathetic nervous system, which regulates arousal and activity, is shifting into the background and that your parasympathetic nervous system, which regulates relaxation and healing, is taking over. Slower, deeper breaths are your body's way of shifting into a more relaxed mode. The same change in breathing patterns automatically occurs when your mind–body prepares to fall asleep at night.

It is no coincidence that hypnotherapists such as Erickson have traditionally used the deeper breath to help people enter a therapeutic trance. They typically tell the patient, for example, "You will take a deeper breath as you close your eyes and go into a hypnotic state." In this sense therapeutic hypnosis facilitates our natural tendency to breathe in a more relaxed manner so that we can access the deeper levels of our natural Ultradian Healing Response.

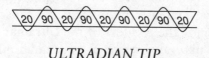

ULTRADIAN TIP

When settling into the Ultradian Healing Response, simply notice your breathing and where the comfort is greatest in your body. By focusing on your comfort wherever it is, you will help it spread throughout the rest of your body. Simply enjoy the calming comfort that deepens as you access your natural Ultradian Healing Response.

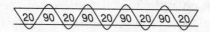

Biologists call this process of cuing the mind–body's natural rhythms *entrainment*. No outside suggestion is needed, however, when we learn to help ourselves by simply recognizing and allowing the Ultradian Healing Response to take place. There is nothing you have to do in this stage of the Ultradian Healing Response. Each naturally gentle breath helps usher you further into the next stage of ultradian healing, where the doors of your inner mind–body begin to open.

Learn to relish and welcome these comfortable healing periods throughout the day when you don't have to think, react, defend, or do things to be in control. Your deepening comfort is nature's signal that many families of messenger molecules (such as the endorphins) are flowing through your mind–body to facilitate healing and well-being.

Stage Three: Mind–Body Healing

In this stage you reach the heart of the Ultradian Healing Response, where the deepest levels of mind–body healing occur. You let yourself float, drift, and simply enjoy, allowing the mind–body to direct its own healing and rejuvenation. You will find your comfort naturally deepening, just as it does when you start to fall asleep for a nap. No conscious effort is needed; just enjoy the comfort of the Ultradian Healing Response, as the natural rhythms of your inner mind–body do the rest.

Each of us experiences this third stage differently. Analytical, logical people have a natural tendency to be absorbed in memories, thoughts, and unfinished business. Right-brain, artistic-intuitive types are inclined to sensations and imagery. Some people experience a kaleidoscope of visual images, dreamlike in their intensity, or find themselves floating in a calming void, empty of feelings, thoughts, sensations, or emotions. There is no right way to experience the third stage. There is no goal to be achieved. You simply tune in to comfort and allow your mind–body to take over and do whatever it needs to revive and restore itself.

The essential feature of this third stage, related to many ancient esoteric practices, is *not doing*: allowing the inner mind–body to do its own work in its own way. At most, you simply witness, quietly and objectively, whatever changes happen by themselves, without acting or reacting to them in any way. This objective witnessing of our inner state and the insights that often accompany it are the beginning of a sense of personal wisdom for many people.

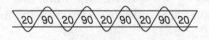

ULTRADIAN TIP

Some mentally active people find—during their first experiences with the Ultradian Healing Response—that racing thoughts and concerns about unfinished business seem to distract them. This is much less of a problem than it would seem. If it happens, simply allow yourself to be aware of what is going on mentally and become more familiar with what thoughts are driving you. As you develop a detached, observing attitude toward these racing thoughts, you will become a bit dissociated from them, and your comfort will deepen all by itself. When you awaken refreshed after about twenty minutes, you may be surprised that you have forgotten how the shift from an overbusy mind to comfort took place. This is a sure sign that you have successfully accessed the healing magic of *not doing*.

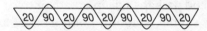

In this stage of the Ultradian Healing Response, while our normally active conscious mind recedes into the background, the real work is done automatically on deeper levels. During these quiet but profoundly healing minutes, the mind–body resynchronizes its many rhythms and systems. Oxidative waste products and free radical molecules that have built up in the tissues during preceding periods of high performance and stress are cleared out of the cells. The stores of messenger molecules so vital to mind–body communication are replenished, and energy reserves are restored.

Psychologically, your mind works to make sense of and integrate the day's experiences. Past experiences, feelings, and events are synthesized into a coherent, stress-free whole, creating new levels of meaning and understanding. This can occur best if you relax and refrain from trying to do anything that requires effort.

This phase of your ultradian rhythm is the deepest window of access to your creative restorative capacity, the core of the Ultradian Healing Response. While it usually takes about twenty minutes, its length will vary widely among different people, or in the same person at different times. Let nature be your guide.

When your mind–body senses it has restored itself to the optimum level for dealing with activity and the stress of life again, you will find yourself moving effortlessly and smoothly into the final stage of ultradian healing: rejuvenated and awakening refreshed.

Stage Four: Rejuvenation and Awakening

As you enter stage four, rejuvenation, you reestablish contact with your normal waking state of mind: You are fully alert again, but calm and refreshed. Your eyes open, and you enjoy a stretch and perhaps a deep breath or two.

Note how supple, smooth, comfortable, and well you feel. This is your mind–body's signal that restoration and healing have taken place. Feeling good is nature's way of saying, "You're doing something right."

This fourth stage is the time when you reap the rewards of your inner journey. You have completed a natural healing period, and your mind–body is beginning its next cycle of optimum performance and activity. The body is now recharged and refreshed. Psychologically, you have allowed the mind to recreate itself so that you awaken with great clarity and acute intuition. You may now know how to deal with a problem with which you had been having difficulty. You may see yourself with greater objectivity, unclouded by the accumulated emotional baggage you took into your ultradian healing break.

Some people may enjoy this feeling so much, they may be tempted to roll right back into another healing ultradian response. They reason that if one is good, then two will be better. Surprisingly, that is not usually so. Unless you are overtired or highly stressed, you are a very different person after the Ultradian Healing Response. Usually, your mind–body will not want to just sit or lie there for another twenty minutes. It starts to engage in thinking, planning, and returning to its usual outer-world focus. You find yourself becoming more and more alert and aroused—your body's way of telling you it is fully revitalized for the activity phase of your ultradian rhythm.

Enjoy this transition to normal waking consciousness for a few minutes, as you move gradually into your accustomed outwardly focused attention. That's all there is to the Ultradian Healing Response: recognition, accessing, mind–body healing, and rejuvenation. The four stages are effortless when you allow nature to do all the work.

The table on the next page contrasts the Ultradian Stress Syndrome and the Ultradian Healing Response side by side for easy reference. Your attitude and willingness to cooperate with your natural life rhythms are what make the difference between them.

FACILITATING YOUR ULTRADIAN HEALING RESPONSE

Given how good the Ultradian Healing Response makes us feel, people are eager to find ways to help themselves move more easily into it. However, the essence of the ultradian approach is not to push or direct but rather to attune yourself to the natural ultradian rhythms of your mind–body. The most effective way to facilitate the ultradian healing response, then, is to simply recognize the natural signals of its onset and allow yourself to enter it when nature calls.

THE ULTRADIAN HEALING RESPONSE

1. Recognition Signals: An acceptance of nature's call for your need to rest and recover your strength and well-being leads you into an experience of comfort and thankfulness.

2. Accessing the Deeper Breath: A spontaneous deeper breath comes all by itself after a few moments of rest as a signal that you are slipping into a deeper state of relaxation and healing. Explore the deepening feeling of comfort that comes spontaneously. Wonder about the possibilities of mind-gene communications and healing with an attitude of "dispassionate compassion."

3. Mind-Body Healing: Spontaneous fantasy, memory, feeling-toned complexes, active imagination, and numinous states of being are orchestrated for healing and life reframing.

4. Rejuvenation and Awakening: A natural awakening with feelings of serenity, clarity, and healing together with a sense of how you will enhance your performance and well-being in the world.

THE ULTRADIAN STRESS SYNDROME

1. Take-a-Break Signals: A rejection of nature's call for your need to rest and recover your strength and well-being leads you into an experience of stress and fatigue.

2. High on Your Hormones: Continuing effort in the face of fatigue leads to the release of stress hormones that short-circuits the need for ultradian rest. Performance goes up briefly at the expense of hidden wear and tear so that you fall into further stress and a need for artificial stimulants (caffeine, nicotine, alcohol, cocaine, etc.).

3. Malfunction Junction: Many mistakes creep into your performance, memory, and learning; emotional problems become manifest. You may become depressed or irritable and abusive to yourself and others.

4. The Rebellious Body: Classical psychosomatic symptoms now intrude so that you finally have to stop and rest. You are left with a nagging sense of failure, depression, and illness.

Nevertheless, there are many ways you can assist yourself in moving naturally into the Ultradian Healing Response:

- If you are feeling hungry, have a light snack containing no more than 200 to 300 calories.

- Gaze out a window at a restful scene.

- Stretch your arms and legs, or take a few deep breaths.

- Massage your neck or back.

- Find a quiet, restful place with subdued lighting, if possible.

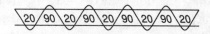

ULTRADIAN TIP

Don't start off with a preconception of what your Ultradian Healing Response should be. We all have unique and highly personal ultradian patterns; become attuned to your own. There is no rigid formula, no right way to experience the response. Although much of our discussion has suggested that the Ultradian Healing Response comes every 90 to 120 minutes and lasts fifteen to twenty minutes, things are rarely so clear-cut in reality. Your personal ultradian rhythms are highly flexible in order to help your mind and body adapt naturally to everything you have to do.

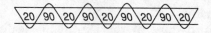

- Lie down, or relax in your chair, and notice what part of your body feels most comfortable. Relax into that comfort and it will spread to other parts of your body.

- Tune in to your natural mind–body rhythms of breathing, heartbeat, and pulse.

- Let your mind wander to a favorite fantasy, image, or restful idea—for example, going on vacation or taking a hike through mountains or meadows.
- Review real life experiences that are comforting.

OTHER BENEFITS OF THE ULTRADIAN HEALING RESPONSE

In addition to the rejuvenating potential of the Ultradian Healing Response, it brings other benefits, especially in its third stage. These include creative insights, vivid daydreams, and what some people call higher or expanded consciousness.

Creative Insights

It is now well established that the unconscious mind is the wellspring of all human creativity. Psychological research by Benjamin Libet at Stanford University and others has shown that our waking perceptions usually lag about two-tenths of a second behind our unconscious mind. We become aware of creative ideas or insights when they bubble up into consciousness from their source in the unconscious. These are the happy moments when we grasp the solution to a vexing problem, suddenly have a new perspective, or are hit with a flash of inspiration. Yet in our usual patterns of rushed everyday life, this creativity breaks through to our waking consciousness only occasionally.

In the third stage of the Ultradian Healing Response, however, the door between waking consciousness and the inner mind opens. When we are focused on the outside world in the active phase of the ultradian rhythm, we may be unreceptive to our inner world of creativity. The outside world of performance demands all our attention. During the ultradian period of inner rejuvenation, we are more sensitive to our inner world and any new and creative ideas that may be developing within.

Accessing your inner mind through the Ultradian Healing Response opens the doors to your creative inner self. You may experience this creativity in many forms: thoughts, visual images, sounds, voices, or even physical sensations. The important thing is to discover your own natural style of inner accessing.

People of all times and cultures have given this ultradian period of creativity many names. Some have termed it the muse, the inner voice, the observing mind, the creative unconscious, the Self, the spiritual guide, an animal totem, the soul, or the anima. Whatever it is called, in the third stage of the Ultradian Healing Response your normal waking consciousness—what psychologists term the executive ego—relinquishes control, allowing the inner, creative parts of your mind–brain to come forward with new patterns of understanding and meaning.

However, try not to pressure yourself to be creative or to recognize new insights. You can hardly expect creativity to flow every time you take an ultradian break! Your mind–body often has other more important inner work to do. If you feel nothing has happened during stage three, trust that your inner mind–body recharging process is proceeding correctly and knows exactly what it needs to do at that moment in order to restore you to your optimum mental, physical, and emotional functioning.

Daydreams

Daydreams are common during the 20-minute ultradian healing break. Some researchers believe the 90-to-120-minute ultradian rhythm is the waking analogue to the same rhythm of our nighttime dreams. As you drift in this comfortable, inner-focused state, you will probably become aware of feelings, memories, images, and thoughts that usually remain locked behind the walls of the occupied rational mind.

These are, in effect, daytime dreams—daydreams. C.G. Jung called our dreams the "the little hidden door in the innermost and most secret recesses of the psyche." The Ultradian Healing Response gives you access to that little door and to the vast potentials of the unconscious mind that exist on the other side of it. However, this inner voice does not follow the rational paths of conscious logic. It may feel intuitive, mystical, random, or disconnected. As in nighttime dreaming, it is precisely the apparent randomness of these daydreams that often leads us to new insights to old problems. The so-called randomness of daydreams actually contains an inner problem-solving logic that the conscious mind does not yet understand.

Altered Experiences of Consciousness

People experienced in using the Ultradian Healing Response often report a feeling of expansive, cosmic consciousness, of seeing the big picture. It is quite common, once you are familiar with ultradian healing, to develop a new sense of meaning and purpose, a fresh outlook on life. Many people experience a greater sense of fitting into the whole, the *gestalt* of interconnection with life and the universe.

Some people who regularly take ultradian breaks sometimes report pleasant out-of-body experiences and a sense of other realities. These experiences suggest a common denominator behind the Ultradian Healing Response and many ancient disciplines of meditation, mindfulness, and higher consciousness. In this sense, esoteric techniques of inner work that lead to such transcendent or transpersonal experiences—including transcendental and Zen meditation, yoga, and even prayer—truly reflect the wisdom of the mind–body utilizing the natural potential for healing, rejuvenation, and transcendence of the limitations of our everyday attitudes.

SOME COMMON QUESTIONS

Most people have many questions about ultradian rhythms and the Ultradian Healing Response. While we don't know all the answers yet, this is what we do know.

What is the difference between an Ultradian Healing Response and a nap?

Everyone's personal experience is so varied that the difference isn't always clear. In general, though, when napping, you actually sleep, descending into a state that registers on a brain-wave (EEG) monitor as delta-wave sleep. That is, your brain waves measure between 0.5 and 4 Hz (herz). In the ultradian state, however, you tend to shift between states of alpha (8 to 14 Hz) and theta (4 to 8 Hz) brain-wave dominance.

Furthermore, when you waken from a nap, you typically do so with a snort and a heavy, slightly groggy feeling that signals you were asleep. When you come out of an Ultradian Healing Response, however, you usually feel comfortable and alert. You have been in another mode of being, somewhere between consciousness and sleep. After an Ultradian Healing Response, unlike a nap, there usually is no residual sluggish feeling, but a relaxed and clear sense of refreshment.

Americans take an average of one or two naps per week, and one-third of the population naps four or more times each week. Your personal experience is your best guide. If a short sleeping siesta is refreshing for you, that may be the best way to experience your after lunch or mid-afternoon ultradian break.

Is there a connection between the Ultradian Healing Response and meditation?

Can it really be a coincidence that most methods of meditation (at least for beginners) all require about twenty minutes? Is it likewise a coincidence that thousands of scientific studies of the various approaches to holistic health, including imagery, meditation, hypnosis, and biofeedback, also use a 20-minute healing period? Although the traditional teachers of meditation and modern researchers never say why they recommend this 20-minute healing period. I believe that they have stumbled upon the same natural 20-minute rest—rejuvenation phase of our 90-to-120-minute basic rest—activity cycle. I therefore hypothesize that the different approaches to meditation and mind—body healing are actually culturally conditioned ways of evoking the same natural 20-minute Ultradian Healing Response.

We can imagine that in the evolution of all these different methods of inner access, there might have been an original genius, a person who was very good at evoking visual images, for example, and then tried to teach his method to all his disciples: "You do it through visual imagery." Perhaps another teacher had a great kinesthetic muscle sense and advocated body massage, while still others through their personal experience found that yoga positions, breathing, sound, and mantras were the key to reaching a healing state.

The problem with these ancient views is they have become formalized in ways that may not fit your individuality. You may be *required* to meditate in a certain posture, on certain images, or with a certain belief system that is not appropriate for you and your background. The Ultradian Healing Response, by contrast, tends to be culture free. It seeks to facilitate healing and well-being by heeding our natural hour-and-a-half life rhythms.

Is the Ultradian Healing Response some form of self-hypnosis?

It is if you believe that when you find yourself wanting to take a break and relax a bit, you are experiencing what some therapists call "The Common Everyday Trance." It is not hypnosis in the sense of trying to program or suggest things to yourself. The Ultradian Healing Response is listening to nature—not trying to tell it what to do.

How is this different from affirmations, autosuggestion, and so on?

The typical world view today is that we need suggestions, programming, and affirmations to tell ourselves what to do. The alternative provided by the Ultradian Healing Response is to listen to the messages from our inner nature when it chooses to talk to us every hour-and-a-half or so.

Why won't a good night's sleep or a relaxed weekend give me the restoration I need?

It actually will give you some of the restoration you need to make up for a lot of ultradian abuse throughout the week. However, people who work hard throughout the week tend to do the same on weekends. How many of us in modern society really use that time for healing and rejuvenation? That is the problem.

How many ultradian healing periods do I really need each day?

All of us have to learn about our own needs. Once you have learned how to appreciate your personal need for Ultradian Healing Responses, you can explore just how many you need to function at your best. Many people find that they work best with two or three 15-to-20-minute ultradian healing breaks each day.

Our needs can be different at different times, however. When a lot of exciting things are happening, you may well forget to take an ultradian break or two. That is perfectly okay. Your mind–body can easily compensate for a few skipped breaks. But remember, you experience a dozen or more ultradian cycles per day, and overriding the Ultradian Healing Response too often will inevitably lead to the Ultradian Stress Syndrome.

It seems impractical for me to schedule an ultradian healing period during my day at work, which just isn't set up to allow for that kind of interruption. What can I do?

In Chapter 6, I will explain ways in which you can use the Ultradian Healing Response at work and offer some alternatives for when you simply cannot find the time for a full break. For now, though, consider the problem in this way: many of us feel that our schedule is not within our control, but there are often times when we simply fail to take control. For example, if you know that you regularly feel a desire for a break around 3:00 P.M., put it into your schedule as if it were an appointment with yourself. If when the time comes you don't feel the desire for a break, you can continue your work in a somewhat less harried manner. But if you do want the break, the time has been set aside for it.

We all tend to overschedule our day, and many people have an opportunity to give themselves a healing moment but fail to take advantage of it. The issue is how well you are able to function without such breaks and how much better you will function if you take them. It is always difficult to set aside time for a new activity in life. A small period of experimentation with Ultradian Healing Responses, however, will convince you that building them into your work schedule is a significant way to enhance your productivity, to say nothing of the physiological and psychological benefits that come from attending to your needs. You simply need to make the determination to do an Ultradian Healing Response whenever it feels right, and then follow through with it.

Will any significant 20-minute break from my schedule give me the benefits of an Ultradian Healing Response? Could I walk in the park or relax myself by reading or watching television for the same amount of time?

Any significant break will give you some ultradian benefits. If your work is sedentary, a relaxing walk could be an ideal way to experience an Ultradian Healing Response.

But why clutter up your mind by reading or watching television when your mind–body is struggling to do its internal bookkeeping? If doing light reading or watching television is the only way you can let yourself take a break, then do so.

But while you are at it, tune in to your feelings of comfort and gradually learn to enjoy them enough that you don't need reading or television as a crutch or a distraction.

Sometimes when I wake up from a 15-to-20-minute ultradian break, I feel more tired than when I sat down for it. What should I do?

When you feel more tired after a 20-minute ultradian break, it means you have more need for rest and rejuvenation than you realized. This is especially true after lunch or in mid-afternoon, when many people take a siesta. Try taking a nap for about an hour. You may also need to get more sleep at night.

If I put my head back and just fantasize for twenty minutes, do I get any ultradian benefits?

Yes, you will experience many natural ultradian benefits. In fact, when you feel like fantasizing it means you are entering the Ultradian Healing Response.

If one of my signals is hunger, is it good to take my snack before or after my break period?

Most people do best by having a snack before the Ultradian Healing Response. A little food will satisfy your natural 90-minute hunger rhythm and signal your mind and body that this is the optimal time for inner healing, restoration, and recovery from the stress of life.

How much before bedtime can I take an ultradian break without disturbing my normal sleep patterns?

Two or three hours. Your normal sleep pattern has its own circadian/ultradian rhythm that shifts among at least four stages of sleep and dreaming every ninety minutes or so.

What is the best way to begin practicing the Ultradian Healing Response on a regular basis?

Just allow yourself to explore how you experience it naturally when you feel like taking a break in normal everyday life. Little by little, you will learn to heed the natural signals your mind–body is sending. As with learning how to drive, the first few trials seem confusing, but then you will take them effortlessly and automatically.

In the beginning, I recommend doing a seven-day ultradian intensive. This is a helpful practice in learning how to access and facilitate the Ultradian Healing Response. It involves paying attention to your ultradian rhythms and recording your experiences in an ultradian diary several times a day for a week.

Here is how to do your ultradian intensive.

1. For seven days, note carefully the signs that you are beginning to enter the Ultradian Healing Response and the times of day at which they occur.

2. If possible, when you become aware of your Ultradian Healing Response cues, take time out and let yourself tune in to where the comfort is, knowing you don't have to *do* anything. Spend about twenty minutes or so enjoying your natural Ultradian Healing Response.

3. After you naturally find yourself coming out of ultradian rejuvenation, note how long you were in it. Notice how you feel, and write a sentence or two about any daydreams, memories, insights, and feelings that occurred. Note whether you resolved any issues or had any new ideas—but don't put yourself under any pressure to do so. For optimal benefit, it may be important that your inner mind–body do its own work without having to tell you about it.

In the ultradian intensive, it is often useful to write down your experience for two reasons. First, it can be very healing to retain a memory of your personal patterns that may become important for self-understanding. Although any one ultradian rejuvenation period is subjective, if you keep a log of such periods for a week, you will begin to create an objective document about what problems and potentials occupy your inner mind—what issues you are dealing with that you might not even be aware of.

With this intensive report, you can then sit down for an objective look at yourself. It provides an inventory of your inner preoccupations. Are the issues clear to you? If not, you may want to record another week of observations. Many people in my research treated themselves to an ultradian intensive every few months, to see what changes have taken place and what new levels of awareness have developed.

Those who did Ultradian Healing Responses every day found that they gradually began to gain broader patterns of insight into themselves and their lives. Many reported a greater sense of comfort with and sensitivity to their own desires, a deeper sense of their core selves. You too may discover that the windows to your inner mind that tend to open during the Ultradian Healing Response can reveal much about your preoccupations and needs. From these inner sessions, you may find you are receiving important hints about how to deal with stresses in your life.

Whatever it brings you, you will get more out of the Ultradian Healing Response if you are willing to fully experience and pay attention to any changes—without demanding that they take place.

5

THE ULTRADIAN TOOLBOX

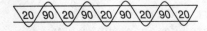

This chapter offers a set of ultradian tools you can use to increase the potential of the Ultradian Healing Response in your life. You may be experiencing difficulties in your job or with your family or mate, you may have symptoms involving stress, sexuality, overeating, or you may have chronic physical complaints. Or perhaps you simply want to explore psychological and spiritual growth.

As you will see, many of these ultradian tools are universal; they have been known in many times and cultures by many different names. Meditation, mindfulness, massage, imagery, hypnosis, psychic healing, biofeedback, and many rituals of shamanism, spiritualism, and prayer all involve tuning in to a natural process of healing. The Ultradian Healing Response reflects the common core of all the holistic approaches to mind–body healing. The more enlightened practitioners of these different approaches humbly admit that they are doing nothing more than giving nature a chance to do the healing. Your ultradian tools are:

1. **Tuning in to your mind–body talk.** This is a natural way of understanding your body's movements, symptoms, sensations, and feelings as channels of communication between your mind and body that can help you in solving problems.

2. Ultradian questions. These focus the inner workings of the mind–body to help you with specific issues of health, performance, and creativity.

3. Accessing and reframing. This is a natural way of breaking through your previous limitations to get in touch with your potentials for effectively resolving emotional and psychological issues of the past and present.

4. The brain–breath connection. This is a new way of learning how to use your breath to balance the left and right sides of your brain to optimize your moods, mental skills, and performance in daily life, work, and sports.

5. Entraining ultradian rhythms. This is a natural and comfortable way of tuning in to your self and others to facilitate family relationships, romance, school, and business.

TUNING IN TO YOUR MIND–BODY TALK

We all experience mind–body talk all the time without knowing it. Every itch, hunger pang, pain, emotion, image, hunch, tension, and desire is a mind–body message. We often have problems with these messages because they seem to come at inconvenient times, and so we tune them out. We try to kill the messenger just because we don't like the message!

The Ultradian Healing Response can be like a mind–body radio tuner. In the quiet, receptive ultradian state we can receive and amplify our natural mind–body messages and allow them to transform themselves into healing and problem-solving clues.

Most of us need to develop a new understanding of and appreciation for the mind–body's natural language. Keeping an ultradian diary can be a key to unlocking the mysteries of your personal style of mind–body talk. Here are some examples from the diaries of people that show how tuning in to our mind–body talk can lead to healing and problem solving during the Ultradian Healing Response.

The first example illustrates the way the Ultradian Healing Response can bring relief even to suffering caused by physical injury. This patient was suffering from serious pain due to a leg and hip injury. Using the ultradian healing response, the patient was able to transform the pain into a mildly sore itch. At one point, he wrote:

> Sensed a moderate to heavy pressure in the hip area. Actually thought that my right foot was resting on left injured side. Went to move it and realized my legs were apart. I concentrated on just tuning in to the pain to learn what would happen. The pain sensation soon dissolved, and I then experienced being able to have the sensation of moving my injured leg in every direction without actually moving it. I experimented with this as it quite fascinated me at the time. The pain of the hurt leg is now more like the mildly sore itch you get when you know you're recovering from a physical injury.

In another case, enhanced mind–body communication during an Ultradian Healing Response helped to resolve a problem between a mother and daughter that apparently was the source of a tension headache.

> I begin with a headache at the base of my skull and then the words from a song come: ". . . what do you mean?" I dimly realized I was still mulling over the events of the day, and I'm angry at my daughter about similar events in the past. I suddenly get a more conscious flash about a communication with my daughter this morning.
>
> Afterward the headache is gone but I now am conscious of an unpleasant tension that tells me I've really got to clear things up by talking them over with my daughter.

In another case, a patient utilized the deep comfort of the Ultradian Healing Response to relieve the stress of a difficult workday.

Upsetting day. Problems with the bank made me come unglued. I went into an unpleasant, tense state when I lay down—anxious and compulsively ruminating about the bank stuff. Then my mind went off to a place of "nowhere." It felt comfortable, sort of like meditation but not even the effort of saying a mantra or doing anything. This is the first time it's happened, and now I feel sort of lucid. Got a new idea about how to handle the bank and feel quite a bit better.

This type of inner mind–body talk and engagement that seems to take place all by itself is a typical way of using the Ultradian Healing Response to deal with nagging, unfinished business.

The two steps for learning how to recognize and facilitate a natural process of mind–body talk are:

1. Receive the message. In the beginning simply pay attention to whatever message arises: buzzing in the ear, toe pain, headache, words from a song, emotional distress, and so on. You may notice a dialogue going on within yourself, as was evident in the case in which the patient "concentrated on just tuning in to the pain, which soon dissolved."

2. Allow spontaneous ultradian shifts between activation and relaxation. Spontaneous and entirely unexpected shifts and transitions may occur in your mind–body messages; they should not be inhibited. For instance, some people may occasionally experience arousal in the initial stage of the Ultradian Healing Response. This may signal the beginning of a spontaneous process of mind–body activation in preparation for problem solving. Soon thereafter they experience a shift to deepening comfort and peaceful feelings that usually follow after they have resolved a problem.

If you try to suggest or program yourself into relaxing in the beginning, as most schools of holistic healing propose, you may actually interfere with these natural processes of problem solving. You may have an illusion of health while simply covering up your problems. This is illustrated by the second case above, where the headache was soon transformed into an insight into the patient's anger about past events and how they might be related to a current communication problem with her daughter. In other systems of healing, people are often told to relax away the tension, but in doing so, they lose the opportunity to experience effortless problem solving and insight.

ULTRADIAN QUESTIONS

Asking ultradian questions is a way of focusing your mind–body talk to approach problem solving during the four stages of the Ultradian Healing Response.

Stage one: recognition. A good time to ask your first question may be during the initial recognition stage of the Ultradian Healing Response. When you find yourself stretching and you decide to take a break, simply wonder what your mind–body wants to deal with. No self-programming is needed! This completely open and nondirective attitude is best, because it gives carte blanche to the vast knowledge base and resources within you.

Stage two: accessing. As you tune in to your sensations, feelings, and breathing during this stage, you may find yourself wondering about the meaning of an ongoing experience. Most schools of meditation tell you to simply note what comes up and then let it go. The constant letting go is what brings you to what some professionals call a therapeutic dissociation, wherein your conscious mind can move toward peace and serenity while your inner mind deals with the issue.

This traditional mindfulness approach is certainly of value. But suppose you find your mind obsessively running back over the same issues again and again? Obviously, your mind–body is stuck with a problem it is desperately trying to solve. This point therefore presents a valuable opportunity to ask your mind–body a few questions about the concerns you might explore. Psychologists call these *accessing questions*.

The essence of initiating this dialogue is a creative wondering with open-ended questions. It is best if these questions invite further exploration and not be answerable with a mere "yes" or "no." Such questioning implies a give-and-take relationship with your inner self. For example, you might say to yourself:

- I wonder how my inner mind will deal with this problem.
- I wonder whether I will have any new thoughts about the impasse at work when I come out of my Ultradian Healing Response.
- I wonder whether my inner mind will give me a definite insight into my problem with overeating.
- I wonder how my inner healer is going to help me cure my headaches/insomnia/ulcers.

All of these are variations of one basic question: "How can my mind–body use all my potentials and previous life experiences to deal with what is going on now?"

When you offer a question to your mind–body, you are opening a dialogue with other parts of yourself. You are initiating a process of mind–body talk that can marshal your inner resources for problem solving and healing. These may include inner resources that your conscious waking mind doesn't even know about.

One problem with overly directive suggestions, and with many of the popular methods of self-programming by subliminal tapes, is that they imply that you should be telling your unconscious what to do. Such directives can be counterproductive. Who among us are so wise that we actually know how to program ourselves and guide the billions of mind–body messages that are continually flowing through us?

The goal here is *not* to think about your problem from

your typical points of view, but rather to just let in ideas, images, and sensations that arise naturally all by themselves. New knowledge and healing possibilities come out of this creative inner dialogue. For that reason, open-ended questions are most useful for commencing a dialogue with the inner self.

This perspective is consistent with the basic philosophy of ultradian healing: we already make too many demands on ourselves. The Ultradian Healing Response is the mind–body's turn to engage in whatever problem solving or healing it feels is most necessary. This is hardly the time for your conscious mind to be in control, giving orders. If your conscious mind knew the answer, would you be having the problem in the first place?

Stage three: mind–body dialogue. During this inner working stage of ultradian healing, you may find yourself engaged in typical patterns of mind–body talk. Alternatively, you may find you really do let go of such self-talk and self-direction once you have posed a satisfactory question to your inner mind that it can deal with by itself. Whichever happens, do not force an issue.

Stage four: rejuvenation. As you begin to experience the fourth stage, rejuvenation, you are again at a window of self-receptivity. At first it is wise to remain still and simply note any obvious and immediate fruits of your inner journey that might be on the verge of becoming available to your conscious mind.

Before you get up and become active again, use this moment to take stock. For example, you might wonder:

- Did my inner mind have some guidance about this issue?
- Is there anything new I see about this situation?
- How might I put that idea into effect?

It is surprising how often the germ of a new idea will be present or that you see an old idea in a new light. Perhaps you had been uncertain about which of many options you should pursue for a personal problem or work issue. Now, for whatever reason, it becomes obvious which course to take.

Again, be gentle. Ultradian questions require the lightest touch, the greatest delicacy. Such self-commands and suggestions as "I have to be a better father/mother" or "I should be less sensitive" are more like demands to be defended against, and as such they can be formulas courting failure. They may start off another cycle of stress. Your path to personal health and well-being lies in gentle, exploratory opening to the new that is constantly developing within you.

To get the most from ultradian questions, remember the following tips:

1. Wait until you are ready. Ultradian questions work best when you are already comfortable in using the Ultradian Healing Response. Only then should you experiment with open-ended questions. Before then, questions may only distract you and disrupt your process of learning to use the Ultradian Healing Response.

2. Hands off is best. It is always wrong to overdirect your Ultradian Healing Response. When in doubt, avoid any form of verbal self-suggestion that might distract your natural process of mind–body communication. The mind–body has access to many sources of information from virtually every cell of the body. We do best by letting it work in its own way.

3. Go gently. Have wonder and compassion, but never program yourself. It is silly to order, command, threaten, cajole, blackmail, or plead with your inner self when it is already trying to do its best.

ACCESSING AND REFRAMING

The third item in the ultradian toolbox is accessing and reframing, a tool that can help you with a variety of mind–body symptoms, particularly those involving physical discomfort and psychological disturbance.

Accessing and creative reframing has its roots in many traditional and non-Western healing disciplines. In the Vispassana branch of Buddhism, for example, the approach dates back several thousand years. More recently it has emerged as a leading idea in the new Ericksonian approaches to hypnosis and psychotherapy.

This tool, like the others, takes special advantage of the restorative pathways open to us during the Ultradian Healing Response. This approach consists of two concepts. Accessing means becoming ultrasensitive and aware of any discomfort or symptom as a useful mind–body signal rather than a problem to be avoided. Creative reframing means finding a broad frame of reference that gives the symptom-signal you are feeling a fuller meaning in your life experience. This approach helps you to recognize your symptoms as guides to healing rather than as annoyances or problems. Instead of experiencing the symptoms in a negative way, you let them become a message, your mind–body's way of telling you where to focus your ultradian healing potential.

How to Access and Creatively Reframe

When you go into your Ultradian Healing Response, be aware of any sensation or symptom you may be feeling. Simply tune in and experience it. Avoid the usual defensive effort to alleviate discomfort; rather, experience it fully. If it seems to momentarily get worse, throbs harder, or becomes more intense, rejoice! You have made strong contact with a symptom or signal reflecting the way your mind–body has encoded the problem.

Now that you have made contact with a problem area, you can experience how it creatively reframes and transforms itself. Does the headache, which was focused in one area, shift slightly? Does the backache expand or contract as you tune into it sympathetically? Does the pain that was localized move up or across your limbs? As the sensation moves, does it soften and grow less intense, like a drop of ink dissolving in a glass of clear water?

It is important to recognize that reframing is a creative experience; that is, you do not do it with your conscious mind. You do not decide ahead of time what form the creative reframing will take—for example, that you will shift the location of pain from one place to another. You do not decide how you will change the quality of your experience of pain into comfort. You simply access the pain and allow your inner mind–body to surprise you with its own creative reframing. The fact that you are surprised by the therapeutic outcome means that it was a genuinely creative experience that you could not have anticipated.

This is the difference between suggestion and programming theories of healing and the ultradian process of accessing and creative reframing. In the suggestion approach, you try to tell the inner mind–body how to respond. You have a plan in your conscious mind and you try to use it to program your inner mind. This assumes that your inner mind is like a huge, sleeping giant that needs suggestion. Most of the methods of self-help found in popular books use suggestions as a form of programming, in which nothing new or creative is involved—you simply try to tell your mind–body what to do.

Why do we need a genuinely new and creative experience to deal with mind–body problems? If there is nothing new and creative in your experience, your symptoms and pains may simply repeat themselves over and over again. This is how stress-related problems become chronic. The accessing and creative reframing approach is therefore particularly appropriate for dealing with old, repetitive, chronic problems.

With the accessing and creative reframing approach, you consciously initiate the access, but you allow your inner mind to do the creative reframing. You access your symptoms by simply tuning in to whatever sensations, feelings or thoughts are associated with them and then wonder how they will be creatively reframed by your inner mind. Within the open window of the Ultradian Healing Response, you allow the inner mind to create its own unique resolution of the problem.

An inspiring example of creative reframing comes from Milton Erickson's life. Erickson experienced chronic arthritic pain in the last decade of his life. He was able to use self-hypnosis to relieve the pain in the daytime, but he would awaken from sleep with pain about every two hours or so throughout the night. This in itself was an ultradian problem, since he was probably awakening out of REM dream sleep, which takes place every 90-to-120 minutes or so during sleep. To reestablish pain relief he would sit up in bed and access the quality and precise location of the pain sensations. On one occasion, he was particularly distressed by a sharp, severe pain that seemed to come from deep within the bones of his shoulder joint. As he accessed this frightening pain, it was suddenly reframed so that he experienced it as a hot wire on the surface of his skin. It now felt as if it were a short, hot wire on the *top* of his shoulder rather than deep within the bone. That was a creative reframing, a gift from his inner mind. Genuinely surprised by this therapeutic transformation, he then experienced the wonderment of how this sharp, hot wire on the surface of his skin gradually faded into warmth as it spread around the shoulder. This, in turn, spread into a feeling of warmth and heaviness throughout his body. At this point he finally found himself drifting into a warm comfortable slumber.

Erickson's wife, Elizabeth, often awakened with him. She reports that her husband's therapeutic process of accessing and creative reframing was not always easily achieved:

> The unconscious may know more than the conscious mind, and should be left to develop its own learnings without interference, but it's not always plain sailing, and it may go about things in the wrong way.
>
> Some of Erickson's experiences with pain control have been trial-and-error, with a good deal of *error*. For example, there have been many long weary hours spent when he would analyze the sensations verbally, muscle by muscle, over and over, insisting on someone (usually me) not only listening but

giving full, absorbed attention, no matter how late the hour or how urgent other duties might be. He has absolutely no memory of these sessions, and I still don't understand them. I feel they were blind alleys, but perhaps they may have involved some unconscious learnings. Then again, maybe not. The reason I mention this is that I think many people might get discouraged when the unconscious gets lost temporarily in a blind alley. The message is "Hang in there. Eventually it will work through."

This example from the personal life of someone who was considered a master of hypnosis helps us realize that accessing and creatively reframing mind–body problems is an art and skill that must be learned through trial and error. There is no magical method that works for everyone every time.

THE BRAIN–BREATH CONNECTION

The brain–breath connection is a versatile tool that can be applied to a wide variety of mind–body issues. To fully understand it, a bit of background is necessary. For a century, modern medical science has known that one of the body's hidden ultradian rhythms is the shift of blood flow between the left and right sides of the nose. As blood flow shifts from one nostril to the other, it affects the size and shape of the inner nose, and hence how easily breath flows in and out of each nostril. When the left nostril opens to permit the easy passage of air, the right nostril is relatively more congested, and vice versa.

It turns out that this long-observed nasal rhythm provides a glimpse into the cerebral hemispheric balance in the brain. While this research is still controversial and there are wide variations in the way different individuals respond, it has been established that when the right nostril is more open, the left brain hemisphere is dominant, and vice versa. (In other words, the nostril that is more congested is on the same side as the currently activated brain hemisphere.) Studies seem to confirm that when the right nostril is more open (indicating left-brain dominance), people perform better on left-brain activities, such as verbal tasks. When the left nostril is more open (suggesting right-brain dominance), subjects perform better on right-brain skills, such as spatial performance tasks.

It is likely that we use this brain–breath connection without realizing it. Almost certainly, we tend to fall asleep while lying on one side or the other. Turning the head to one side is an instinctive way of changing the nasal balance. As we do, we change the body's autonomic nervous-system balance from the arousal-producing sympathetic nervous system to the relaxation-producing parasympathetic system, thus preparing the brain for sleep. Perhaps the insomniac's tossing and turning is an unconscious attempt to find the optimal brain–breath relationship for sleep.

The first step in using this tool is to check your current hemisphere balance. Here are three ways you can ascertain it.

1. Mirror condensation method. This simple method is often used by yoga breathing experts. Hold a small pocket mirror under your nose perpendicular to your face. Breathe naturally through the nose on to the mirror for a few seconds. The pattern of water vapor from your breath on the mirror reveals which nostril is more open—the smaller the blot, the more congested the nostril, suggesting that same side of the brain is likely to be dominant. Experiments show this method is accurate 92 percent of the time.

2. Exhaling sound method. Close one nostril with gentle thumb pressure on the opening. Exhale short and sharply through the open nostril, noting the sound. The greater the congestion, the higher pitched the exhaling sound. Do the same with the other nostril, alternating back and forth a few times to hear the difference. The nostril giving the higher pitch is more congested, suggesting that same side of the brain is currently more highly activated.

3. Tactile sensation method. This method requires a bit of practice. Take in a deep, slow breath through your nose, paying attention to which side feels more open and which more congested or stuffy. With a little practice, many people find that they can reliably tell which side is more congested. That is the side of the brain that is dominant.

Lying down is the simplest way to shift nasal balance. If you lie on the side with the more open nostril for a few minutes, a physiological reflex will make the blood flow into the tissues of the nostril on the down side, congesting it. This, in turn, shifts your brain-hemisphere dominance to that side. Clinical experience suggests that this shift by itself is often enough to change mood and psychosomatic symptoms.

You can use a variety of positions to facilitate the brain–breath connection. (See Figure 3.) You begin by using a neutral position to observe what your current brain–breath relationship is. In the neutral positions A, B, and C there is no effort to shift brain–breath dominance.

Lying on the left side, as in position D, tends to close the left nostril and open the right. This, in turn, reflexively tends to activate the left hemisphere of the brain with its more verbal, analytical skills. Lying on the right side, as in position E, tends to activate the right side of the brain with its more holistic, spatial, and emotional skills. These are only general guidelines, however. You need to explore just how the brain–breath link is related to your own styles of thinking, feeling, and being.

The following example from a young woman's ultradian diary illustrates how she received an important spontaneous insight into the connection between her headaches and her relationship with her boyfriend, when she shifted her brain–breath balance by lying on her right side.

I felt very resistant to taking a break, even though it was three in the afternoon and I had not rested all day. Thoughts of things I have to do or should be doing. I try to just let these

Position A
Lying flat on back

Position B
*Sitting down straight
in a chair*

Position C
Lotus position

Position E
Lying on right side of body

Position D
Lying on left side of body

FIGURE 3. *Shifting the nasal–brain correspondence. Positions A, B, and C
are neutral positions in which the Ultradian Healing Response can optimize
rest and rejuvenation by allowing the nasal–brain rhythm to find its own
appropriate balance. Position D, with the left side of the face down, facilitates
the opening of the right nostril and activates the left side of the brain for
outer-directed and intellectual work. Position E, with the right side down,
facilitates opening the left nostril and activating the right side of the brain for
inner work and artistic types of experience. Yogis traditionally recommend
sleeping on the right side at night. (From "New Yoga of the West,"* Psychological Perspectives, *Volume 22, 1990.)*

thoughts be, but I can't let go. My breathing became more shallow and I worried about not being comfortable. I realize I'm lying on my left side, which may be turning on my left analytical brain, so I turn and lie on my right side. After a few moments I have a quiet thought that seems significant: My headache occurs more frequently when I have something to say that might not be agreeable to my boyfriend. I'm surprised that my eyes become tearful. I come fully awake thirty minutes later with a groggy but comfortable feeling.

The brain–breath tool is an effective one, and we will come back to it in subsequent chapters as we explore how to use the Ultradian Healing Response for physical and emotional problems at work and in our personal relationships.

ENTRAINING ULTRADIAN RHYTHMS

The final item in the ultradian toolbox is entrainment. It is not so much a specific how-to tool as a phenomenon that operates in a myriad of ways in our daily encounters with others. Once we understand it, entrainment can help us have more productive and harmonious relationships.

Entraining happens when we receive cues that bring our internal ultradian rhythms in line with other people or events in our environment. When light dawns and we wake up, when darkness makes us feel like sleeping, when we see a platter of steaming food and want to eat, or when we find ourselves in sync with our lovers, we are being entrained by environmental cues.

Among the most powerful entrainers of our circadian and ultradian rhythms are the people around us. This entraining is a process of getting in synchrony with one another. Any time we send or receive social cues, whether conscious or unconscious, that bring our ultradian status more in sync with another person's, entrainment is taking place. You might think of entraining as entwining one person's ultradian rhythm with another's.

Though we may not have realized it, everyday social relationships are an endless procession of psychosocial entraining cues. We constantly give and receive signals that reflect and affect our own ultradian status and that of others. For example, one person yawns, and immediately several others nearby do the same; a friend says, "I'm going to grab a bite to eat," and you notice you are beginning to feel hungry. These social and psychological cues are actually changing our physiology by the process of ultradian entrainment. This is one of the fundamental ways that mind can affect the body. As we emphasized earlier, this is the way the entrainment of ultradian rhythms can bridge the so-called mind–body gap.

Because our ultradian rhythms are so flexible and responsive to what is going on around us, others can easily entrain us into either an ultradian trough or peak. The preacher who says, "Now let us pray" entrains the congregation into a state of inner contemplation and healing as they fall into the body's natural Ultradian Healing Response. The hypnotherapist who tells a client to relax into a therapeutic trance does the same. Even so ordinary an act as stroking a dog or cat can reduce our stress and tension. The pet's pleasure and relaxation when being petted entrains us into our own Ultradian Healing Response!

Just as easily, we can be moved into ultradian peaks. The coach who lathers the team into fighting spirit before the big game, the orator whose fiery harangue whips a crowd to a tumultuous frenzy, and the professor whose infectious excitement inspires her students all are entraining their audience to top performance.

Food: The Edible Entrainer

The act of eating with others is a powerful entrainer that can put our ultradian rhythms in sync with another's. Regardless of where we may be in our ultradian rhythm, the sight or smell of food is a cue that entrains our 90-to-120-minute hunger rhythm. When we satisfy that urge by eating with another person, both of us reset our rhythms together and fall into mind–body synchrony on a variety of levels.

This may be why breaking bread together is inherently such an important sociobiological act, woven deep into our genetic fabric. Many of the world's cultures, from Arab to Italian to Japanese, place a strong emphasis on long, shared meals. In many cultures, two- and three-hour meals are not uncommon and are often linked to the conduct of business. The ultradian synchrony of these events helps ensure that people are closely linked on many mind–body levels and in a mutually receptive state for enhancing relationships and business. When we schedule meetings over meals, we are not merely saving time; we are bonding on a deep mind–body level as we entrain and synchronize our ultradian rhythms with one another's.

Entrain Yourself Out of Jet Lag

You can put your new knowledge of entraining to practical use in a number of ways. For example, you can use it to reset your inner clock and entrain yourself out of jet lag the next time you travel. Most people who fly across several time zones feel hungry at bedtime, sleepy at noon, and generally cranky, disoriented, and mildly out of sorts. This is no wonder, as the body's rhythms are completely out of sync with the switching around of external entraining cues. It is dawn when your inner rhythms expect it to be dark; dinner is served when your body expects breakfast; people are working when they should be home sleeping. With all the cues coming at the wrong times, the jet-lagged mind–body feels discombobulated for several days, until gradually the ultradian rhythms adjust and resynchronize themselves with the cues in the new environment.

You can carefully entrain yourself before, during, and after travel to minimize jet-lag effects. The main rules are simple.

1. Modest fasting for a few days before the journey will intensify the resetting effect of mealtimes in the new locale.

2. Awaken early on the day of the flight, to increase your need for sleep when you arrive.

3. Drink plenty of fluids—but no alcohol—before and during the flight, to counter dehydration.

4. Keep in-flight stimuli low during hours when people at your destination would be sleeping.

5. Meals in the new locale should be ample to send your body a strong resetting signal. They should be high in protein in the morning, and high in carbohydrates at night.

6. Try to be exposed to three to four hours of sunlight on the first day at your destination; this will have a strong resetting effect on your rhythms.

7. Your physical activity in the new locale should reinforce the local schedule strongly. For example, go to bed, rise, and eat meals according to the time of day at your destination.

8. Caffeine advances the body-clock, but only when drunk late in the day; in the morning it moves it backward.

Try these simple rules on your next vacation or business trip. You may be amazed how much more easily you can reset your energy and sleep schedules by working with your body's rhythms.

The example below was developed by the scientific team of Ehret, Groh, and Meinert at the Argonne National Laboratory in Illinois. It uses food, caffeine, and daylight to help ease the jet lag of a trip from New York to Paris, which involves a time difference of six hours.

Three days before departure: Eat heavily, no caffeine (coffee, cola, tea) in the morning or evening (late afternoon is okay).

Two days before departure: Eat lightly, no caffeine in the morning or evening (late afternoon is okay).

One day before departure: Eat heavily, no caffeine in the morning or evening (late afternoon is okay).

Day of departure: Awake earlier than usual. Eat very lightly, with protein for breakfast and lunch, carbohydrate for dinner. Fruit is okay, but keep daily calories very low. No caffeine all day.

On the flight: Do not eat meals served on the plane. Do not eat any snacks, sugar, or cream. If caffeine keeps you awake, avoid it; if not, drink two or three cups of black coffee or tea. Keep social interaction to a minimum. Turn off the light over your seat. Don't watch the in-flight movie. Relax, try to sleep.

Upon Paris arrival: Eat a large, high-protein breakfast immediately. Eat a large, high-protein lunch on Paris time. Eat a large, high-carbohydrate dinner on Paris time. Exercise, walk, be active—do not sleep in the daytime. No caffeine all day. Be in bed by 10:00 P.M. Paris time (you'll want to be).

Day after arrival: Eat three full meals on Paris time: high-protein breakfast, high-carbohydrate dinner.

You now possess a basic set of ultradian tools. Remember that although ultradian rhythms are eminently flexible and easily shifted, your own inner ultradian cues are your best signals to your actual mind–body state. Always, the most basic of ultradian truths is to heed your body's cues for outer performance and inner healing.

6

MAXIMIZING
PERFORMANCE:

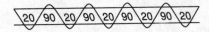

Ultradians and the Worlds of Work, School, and Sports

Most of us spend more than half of our waking hours seeking to accomplish, to achieve, to do—at work, in school, or in sports. Sensitivity to our mind–body cues can help us make that time fulfilling and productive. In this chapter, you will see how our understanding of ultradian and circadian rhythms and the utilization of the Ultradian Healing Response can help us improve our performance. By being aware of ultradian-related shifts in your thinking, mood, and behavior, you can enhance your productivity, creativity, and effectiveness.

THE ULTRADIAN AT WORK

Today, an unprecedented number of Americans make their living with their minds in service- and information-related jobs. Such work requires alertness, high mental capacity, good memory, and interpersonal skills. Those cognitive capacities, of course, are exactly the ones most affected by ultradian rhythms. As was noted earlier, research has shown that our verbal and spatial skills, eye–hand coordination, short-term memory, mental alertness and vigilance, imagination and creativity, concentration, and learning are all affected by the ultradian rhythms of the mind–body.

The echo of our inborn ultradian patterns is clearly evident from our earliest school days to our current workplaces. Look closely at the schedules of our nation's factories, offices, and businesses. The typical American workday is broken into ultradian periods of approximately 90 to 120 minutes, interspersed with short breaks:

7:00–7:30	Wake up
8:30–9:00	Arrive at work
10:30	Snack or coffee break
10:45–12:15	Work
12:15	Lunch
1:30	Back from lunch
3:30	Break
5:15–5:30	Leave work

Unfortunately, many work environments do not respect this natural pace of work and rest. Some employers still act as though everyone is able to function at a perpetually optimum pace, hour after hour. They try to keep us to rigid schedules and time clocks, measuring our worth by how many widgets we produce or how many sales we make by our deadline. How well we feel, how well we work, and whether we are respecting the natural imperatives of our mind–body scarcely enter into the equation. So seduced are we by outer accomplishment that we utterly neglect our vital need for inner restoration. In the headlong pursuit of success, we disrupt the very ultradian rhythms that could help us achieve it.

There is, however, an alternative. As Nathaniel Kleitman, whose pioneering work on the 90-minute basic rest–activity cycle pointed to the idea of the 20-minute Ultradian Healing

Response, suggests, "We can perhaps utilize the existence of this 'biological hour' to schedule classes in schools, work in factories and offices, . . . in general arrange our activities on a rational physiological basis." Right now, in your own life, you can use your growing knowledge of ultradian rhythms to enhance your performance during your workday. You can apply it to:

- know when you are at your peak efficiency for learning and working
- perform optimally at important meetings or events
- recognize others' periods of strength and weakness
- recognize early warning signs of errors or accidents at work
- maximize creativity and minimize stress
- reduce burn-out in creative, managerial, and care-giving professions
- create a more nurturing school or work environment

PLANNING FOR PEAKS AND TROUGHS

We all work better and more efficiently when we are not fighting our natural mind–body rhythms. Knowing that your ultradian rhythms constantly affect your mind–body performance throughout every working day, it is wise to plan your activities in advance whenever possible. The surest way to increase enjoyment and productivity at work is to structure your activity to complement your natural mind–body cycles.

Maximum performance rests on this simple dictum: "peak your peaks and trough your troughs." This alternation can bring remarkable improvement in your outer performance as well as your inner health and well-being.

At the peak of your ultradian rhythm, you are in a state of

high activity that is ideal for learning and performance. Sensations and perceptions are sharp and clear. Sensory, motor, and physical performance are at their peak. You move, speak, and think faster and are generally more alert. By knowing when you enter this phase, you can put yourself in top form when you need to be: for that big meeting, for pitching a new client, or for a creative push on an important project.

In the trough, or ultradian recovery phase, most of your sensory and perceptual functions slow down as the mind–body turns inward to do its housekeeping. This is when you experience your personal cues to take a 20-minute break. You become inefficient in outer-world tasks, careless, and prone to errors. The clerk makes a mathematical mistake; the executive erases a crucial computer file; the sales associate dealing with a client becomes irritable and inattentive.

If you persist in trying to work through your troughs, you can fall into the Ultradian Stress Syndrome. People who consistently try to plow through the low point of their natural ultradian rhythms cannot help but sacrifice their peaks. Peaks are for good outer performance; troughs are for good inner healing and inspiration. If you do not take advantage of both the highs and the lows, you disrupt your natural rhythm and fall into what is termed *low-amplitude dysrhythmia*. This simply means that, because you neglect the lows, you never get the rejuvenation needed for the next peak. The lack of ultradian restoration leaves you with a deficit so that you don't have the energy to carry yourself forward to the next natural peak. Performance mediocrity can result.

In order to realize the full range of your capacities and perform at your peak, it is essential that you do the right things at the right times. That means working with complete focus and attention in your peak phase and allowing thorough rest and restoration to occur during the ultradian healing phase.

Take advantage of your natural peaks and troughs, and plan your day accordingly. Here are some suggestions for ways to do this.

Maximize Your Peaks

When you are naturally at your best you feel *on*—alert, your memory and thinking clear and fast, and your body comfortable, functioning automatically and well. Your motor skills are fine and sure, your senses acute. You enjoy a full sense of absorption in your work. You are observant; you take an inherent sense of pleasure and satisfaction in problem solving; and your curiosity, sense of wonder, and thinking skills are aroused.

Transpersonal psychologists call this state *flow*. If we take time to give ourselves the 20-minute rejuvenations we need, these peaks of flow will occur naturally as many as three or four times each day. Other parts of the workday should be dedicated to supporting these peak times. To get the most out of the peak of an ultradian rhythm:

- do something you really love, focusing on those tasks that inspire you and intrinsically motivate you
- do the part of your work you find most creative and challenging
- do highly demanding, motivating activities

In addition, many people find they can optimize their peaks with music, lighting, and other supportive sensory stimulation. From the drumbeats of native societies to modern tapes for synchronizing the brain's hemispheres, strongly rhythmic music has long been recognized as an entrainer or pacer of the mind–body's natural rhythms.

Another powerful way of enhancing your peak performance may be working with a team on a group project. Under ideal conditions the members of the team entrain one another, peaking their activity together and then enjoying let-down periods together as they collectively take a break in preparation for the next peak.

Planning for Meetings

Schedule vital meetings so the most important part will coincide with one of your peaks. Save your nonpeak times for less vital meetings where you don't play a central role. For example, if someone asks you, "Can you meet with me in five minutes to discuss a new approach on the XYZ account?" note where are you in your ultradian rhythm. Are you feeling the signs of ultradian fatigue or even the beginning of the Ultradian Stress Syndrome? Maybe your response should be, "Sorry, I need more lead time. Let's do it in half an hour." This gives you thirty minutes to take advantage of the full Ultradian Healing Response. Then, with your mind–body refreshed and entering an ultradian peak, you just might come up with a new angle for the meeting.

If a meeting lasts longer than ninety minutes, suggest a recess. Chances are every participant will be fatigued and worn out. Also, do not schedule demanding events or meetings back to back without allowing 15-to-20-minute breaks. You need to attend to your ultradian rhythms to restore your maximal functioning and marshal your interpersonal and creative faculties after building up stress and fatigue during a demanding event.

In addition to planning your own time, consider your colleagues' schedules. Determine your associates' typical ultradian patterns. If a co-worker is essential to a project, try to determine that person's peak times: is she a lark or an owl? Then schedule appointments and meetings to take advantage of your associate's peak periods as well as your own.

Shift Your Peaks

It is possible to modify your natural ultradian rhythms to some extent, although this is not highly recommended. You might, for example, want to avoid entering an ultradian trough just as you start a major business presentation. Or you might want to be at your peak before a particularly sensitive negotiation.

In such cases, you can use the nasal shifting tool explained in Chapter 5. Suppose a crucial meeting, which will demand the clear, logical thinking of left-hemisphere function, starts at 3:00 P.M. Forty-five minutes before the meeting, take an ultradian healing break, lying on your right side to help facilitate the brain's cycling into the right (more creative, pattern-recognition) hemisphere. As you relax, you may gently wonder whether your unconscious mind will offer you insights into the key issues before or during the meeting. At 2:45 or so, turn over to your left side. After a few minutes, that more analytical and verbal side of the brain will be more highly activated, preparing you to present yourself at your best. Finally, spend the last few minutes before the meeting reviewing the key issues, noting whether your inner mind has brought up any new ideas. By the time you walk into the meeting, you will be primed for peak functioning.

Similarly, if you have an important meeting early in the morning, you might try going to sleep a half-hour earlier than usual and setting your alarm to awaken a half-hour early. You will thus reset your ultradian rhythms, ensuring you will be at your peak for the meeting. Enjoy the extra half-hour you now have to daydream in bed about your meeting. Simply let yourself receive whatever thoughts and hunches arise. Your creative mind may provide you with new inspiration during such moments.

Heal Yourself During Your Troughs

When you become aware of the mind—body signals that you are entering a trough, follow the four steps of the Ultradian Healing Response in Chapter 4. Give yourself permission to use this time as nature instructs you. In the beginning, it may be difficult to take control of your time and schedule an ultradian break into a busy calendar, but if you experiment a bit you will discover the improvement in your productivity, creativity, and efficiency that the Ultradian Healing Response will yield.

One simple way to begin might be to use a portion of your lunch hour for an ultradian break. As mentioned earlier, you might also block out your calendar for an appointment with yourself during those times of the day when you know you usually feel a need for a break. Then, when that time arrives, you have the choice of taking an ultradian break or continuing your work.

If you are unable to take a break and feel that you need to continue working, keep a pile of nondemanding tasks on your desk. Most jobs consist of a variety of tasks, some more mundane and rote than others. These less important jobs—filing memos, sending invoices, making routine calls—must get done sometime. Turn to them for a change of pace when you must work through your troughs. Why waste precious peak moments of high energy and clear concentration on less important work?

Some people find it useful to keep paper and pen at hand to jot down ideas when they come out of a 20-minute break. This helps them retain any creative insights that may have come up during the Ultradian Healing Response. Most of us have experienced times when we had a sudden brilliant idea that we were sure could solve a problem and have told ourselves the idea is so clear that we can write it down later. But when we try to return to it later, we find our inspiration has vanished. We have lost the energy behind what was originally so exciting.

What happened? In all likelihood, when we first got the idea our brain–body probably already was making its ultradian shift from the less verbal right hemisphere to the more verbal left hemisphere (or some unique combination of both). By ignoring the urgency to write down or express the good idea, we missed the optimal mind–body–brain ultradian moment of creativity. Inspiration may come at the oddest times, but we need to heed the call if we are to follow our inner creativity as it goes through its natural ultradian cerebral shifts.

This ultradian alternation of mental skills has been documented in a classical study in *Science* in 1979. Raymond Klein and Roseanne Armitage of the Department of Psychology at Dalhousie University in Canada reported 90-minute rhythms in human cognitive style. The peaks in verbal and spatial skills clearly alternate with each other every hour-and-a-half or so. These spontaneous ultradian alternations in mind–brain skills may account for many of the mysteries of human creativity and ingenuity. (See Figure 4.)

Manage the Breaking Point

At about 3:00 or 4:00 P.M. most of us enter the time of day that two Japanese ultradian researchers, Yoichi Tsuji and Toshinori Kobayshi, have called the breaking point. In charting brain-wave readings throughout the day, they found two distinct kinds of rhythms: the regular ultradian rhythms, which they clocked at about 100 minutes, and a longer circadian rhythm that changes once in the course of a workday. The breaking point occurs when the low phases of ultradian and circadian rhythms coincide, reinforcing each other. The longer rhythm begins to move us down the long, many-houred slide toward the day's deepest recuperative period, sleep, while a shorter ultradian rhythm is also hitting its low. The result is one of the deepest lows in the day's functioning. The breaking point is experienced as that feeling of deep fatigue we all know in the afternoon as we yawn, stretch, and glance at the clock, wishing quitting time would come.

The Israeli researcher Peretz Levie has also noted this midafternoon dip in alertness that "divides the habitual waking day into two zones: the morning–midafternoon zone, characterized by rapid rhythms in alertness, with a dominant

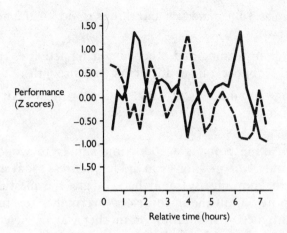

FIGURE 4. *Our alternating verbal and spatial skills. This graph illustrates our natural ultradian alternation of verbal (left-brain) and spatial (right-brain) skills. The solid line indicates performance on verbal left-hemisphere skills; the dotted line indicates performance on spatial right-hemisphere skills. (Adapted from Klein and Armitage, 1979.)*

periodicity of about 90–100 minutes, and the midafternoon–evening zone, characterized by an overall increase in the level of sleepiness. This latter zone is ended by a rather abrupt change in alertness which corresponds to the onset of the rest phase of the circadian cycle."

At breaking point we are not at our best for outer activity, our socializing capacities are relatively weak (with the exception of those owls who become more alert and sociable in late afternoon and evening), and our body's demands for ultradian recuperation become harder to ignore. It is best to follow this low point in your daily cycle with a series of nurturing, restorative activities, such as a favorite hobby, light socializing, reading, listening to music, and meditation. When you experience the breaking point at work, you can:

- take your deepest 20-minute ultradian break of the day (perhaps even a nap if you need one)

- organize your materials and things to do for the next day's work
- engage in reading and other nurturing activities that gently support you but do not tax your strength
- engage in nonstressful conversation or quiet activity with an ultradian-aware co-worker

The breaking point is a good time simply to wonder about the issues and questions you did not address today and will face in the morning. By doing that, you give the questions time to gestate within the unconscious overnight. You may wake up with a creative solution or another way of viewing the situation, thanks to the work of your inner mind.

Some people may even want to schedule an ultradian break into the end of their work day before going home. Not only might this remove you from rush-hour traffic, it can also have a positive impact on your emotional and mental state before you return home to family and personal demands.

WHEN YOU CAN'T TAKE A 20-MINUTE BREAK

Left undisturbed under ideal circumstances, the Ultradian Healing Response usually lasts about fifteen to twenty minutes. But in the hectic push–pull of the real world, taking that kind of time is obviously not always practical. In many job situations it may seem nearly impossible to put the ultradian principles into practice.

One key virtue of the Ultradian Healing Response, however, is that it is adaptable to circumstances. Just because you can't always take the full 20-minute break your mind–body needs, you don't have to lose out on all its benefits. Try one of the alternatives described below.

The Mini Ultradian

Many people have found that they don't need the entire twenty minutes to feel restored by the Ultradian Healing Response; a 3- or 5-minute break may be enough. These mini ultradians can be surprisingly effective.

One executive secretary, for example, found that she would occasionally phase out for two or three minutes during the day as she sat at her desk. Co-workers would notice that in these mini ultradians she stared out the window or at her computer terminal, but she appeared so lost in deep thought that no one dared bother her at such moments. She would then spontaneously come to with a blink or two and a little shake of her head, and move on efficiently to her next task.

For some people, these mini ultradians seem to work well as a substitute for the longer restorative breaks; others find that they need the longer breaks to really feel refreshed. In this, as in all things ultradian, we are all different and must listen to our own mind–body cues and signals.

The Active Ultradian

When you can't afford to take even a short, quiet break in your work environment, there are still ways of gaining some benefit from the Ultradian Healing Response. Any break in concentrated work or distraction from what you have been doing brings some restorative relief.

You may be taking an active ultradian when you find yourself puttering or doodling, talking to a colleague, making a personal phone call, on a short walk through the office, stretching and taking a few deep breaths, or doing routine filing or reorganization tasks. You probably naturally switch to these change-of-pace activities every day. When you do, you are unconsciously responding to the take-a-break signals generated by your ultradian rhythms. These activities are enjoyable because they give your mind–body the chance it needs to replenish messenger molecules and rebalance the brain hemispheres and nervous system.

The key to turning these activities into meaningful ultradian healing breaks, however, is to avoid doing anything difficult, strongly goal-directed, or requiring concentration. That means that certain activities don't work during an active ultradian break: strenuous exercise, self-improvement tasks, programmed or rushed activities, highly directive mind work, operating machinery, time-pressure tasks, decision making, and new creative work.

After a few weeks of learning to use two or three restful Ultradian Healing Responses throughout the day, Allen, an account executive with an advertising firm, reported that he could not always get his mind to rest during his ultradian breaks. In spite of his best efforts to let go during his break, Allen remained aware that his inner mind was still busy humming in the background. He found himself wondering what it was doing. Was it dealing with his current work? Then, sure enough, an incredibly good idea would suddenly pop up on whatever matter he was stuck on at work. It might be the perfect turn of phrase for some advertising copy, or a new way of wording a hidden implication or beguiling question to "catch the fabric of the consumer's mind," as Allen put it. So good were some of these unbidden inspirations that he just had to reach over from his office couch and note them briefly on a writing pad.

Allen would then lie back and continue tuning in to the comfort and well-being of the Ultradian Healing Response. But he was feeling a little guilty about this, worried that he was doing something wrong by letting his work intrude when he was supposed to be relaxing. In fact, Allen need not have worried that he was not really doing ultradian healing the right way. Allen had simply encountered another creative facet of the Ultradian Healing Response: the active ultradian wherein the inner mind–body continues its creative work on outer world tasks.

Activity Shifting

Another way you can still derive real benefit without a full 20-minute break is by shifting your activity to something wholly different from what you have been doing. The goal is to change your mental pace. Simply by treating yourself to a clear change of pace every hour and a half or so, you enjoy a measure of the internal restoration of the Ultradian Healing Response while continuing to work.

Someone who works at intense left-brain intellectual tasks needs some balance by activating the right hemisphere. Those who are usually engaged in an activity requiring gregarious and intensive contact with a lot of people—such as sales or teaching—may feel the need for a solitary break. A high-performance worker, dealing with ringing phones or a demanding interpersonal environment will most likely seek withdrawal and quiet. Those whose jobs are physically sedentary may want to get up and go for a short walk, in a quiet place if possible. A stroll in a park, by a lake, or on a beach is ideal.

One caveat: These three types of substitute ultradian breaks don't completely replace the need for a 20-minute Ultradian Healing Response. Especially when you first begin to apply ultradian principles, taking the full 20-minute break is the best way to get the full benefit of ultradian rejuvenation. Really taking time out and lying down helps reinforce the idea that this is a special and worthwhile oasis of calm in the demands of the day. No matter how experienced you grow in ultradian healing, make time for at least one or two full ultradian healing breaks every day.

THE IDEAL ULTRADIAN WORKPLACE

A truly ultradian-aware workplace would resolve many problems: job dissatisfaction and burn-out, poor performance and morale, union complaints, accidents, stress-related disability, high turnover, and absenteeism. Physically, such a workplace would be designed to maximize opportunities for employees to heed their need for ultradian restoration. Psychologically, managers would understand it is in the best interests of the company to respect the individual's ultradian needs and rhythms. Ethically, employees and employers would enter into a mutually beneficial contract where the job always gets done in an optimal manner because everyone performs at his or her best during their ultradian peaks, and where everyone benefits from personal healing and well-being.

The Ultradian Office

The ideal ultradian office would be designed to allow more employees quiet offices, with floor-to-ceiling partitions to cut down noise and increase privacy. Or they might set aside a quiet, comfortable room with couches or cots behind curtained partitions. Provision would be made to hold telephone calls and interruptions for short periods when an employee felt an Ultradian Healing Response coming on.

One group of privileged people already enjoy such ultradian perks: executives. They usually have private, comfortable offices where they can close the door to lie down or rest. It is no secret that many high achievers often take quick, refreshing breaks in the privacy of their inner sanctums, informing co-workers to hold their calls for fifteen or twenty minutes. By trial and error, they have found that these breaks nurture their health, creativity, and productivity.

What few people have realized is that every employee's health, creativity, and productivity can be enhanced by ultradian principles, with a corresponding benefit to the company. Dr. Candace Pert, former chief of the Section of Brain Biochemistry at the National Institute of Mental Health, has already put these ultradian principles into practice. In her new private laboratory, Integra, her co-workers have access to what she calls a Zen room, a quiet, solitary place where employees are encouraged to take restorative breaks when they feel the need. This enlightened attitude may explain why this laboratory is doing some of the world's most creative work on AIDS, psychobiology, and brain biochemistry.

The Enlightened Ultradian Manager

There is no more important element to the new ultradian workplace than the attitude of the managers, supervisors, and executives who set the tone for the whole organization. Having an ultradian-aware boss is the key to forging a more humane and productive workplace. When managers become knowledgeable about ultradians, they will come to reap the increases in productivity, work quality, and morale it brings. There are three basic tenets for the ultradian-enlightened manager to keep in mind:

1. Tolerance for individual variation in performance is the keystone of the ultradian workplace. To force employees to work on a rigid, externally imposed schedule that supposedly reflects corporate priorities is to fight against our natural processes of rejuvenation, health, and well-being. Doing so sets up a vicious cycle of stress, burn out, and loss of optimum performance that actually undermines corporate priorities.

2. When you see your employees taking a break, know that they are not just wasting time, being lazy, or daydreaming. Don't worry that you are not getting your money's worth. These ultradian breaks will help workers access more creative ideas, make fewer errors, have fewer accidents, decrease absenteeism and personnel problems, and increase job longevity. The Ultradian Healing Response will help the bottom line.

3. Utilize ultradian entrainment. Learn how to recognize the cues that synchronize people into optimum ultradian periods of activity and rest. Getting employees inspired for a sales conference, motivating the whole office into an ultradian peak to meet a deadline, pausing for a pep talk, and even going out to eat together all serve to synchronize employees' ultradian rhythms of optimum performance.

Dr. Bruce Gregory, a psychologist who works with corporate leaders, reports that executives who are able to tap into their ultradian fluctuations are able to facilitate better interpersonal communication within stressful and high-pressure environments by being more effective in the following ways: first, being more comfortable and relaxed themselves; second, being better able to evaluate other people's needs for comfort, reassurance, and information; third, being better able to respond to others' needs by being more sensitive in terms of asking questions that reduce feelings of insecurity and defensiveness in the listener; and fourth, making statements that facilitate cooperative as rather than antagonistic communication, attitudes, and behavior.

In our work lives, we face responsibilities and challenges on every side. To meet them we will need every ounce of strength, our sharpest wits and faculties, and our most passionate commitment. By working with our ultradian rhythms instead of against them, we can ensure that we are functioning at our optimum when we need to be and recuperating for further efforts when our mind–body requires it. Ultradian restoration is one of the most essential tools we have for maximizing personal and professional performance.

APPLYING ULTRADIAN KNOWLEDGE FOR DIFFERENT OCCUPATIONS

Each kind of job has its own ultradian concerns, and people in different occupations may apply the principles of ultradian healing differently. Virtually every occupation has its own demands and scheduling problems, but in every case getting the needed ultradian rejuvenation is the best way to assure maximum, efficient performance. Here are some relevant ultradian considerations for different occupations.

Industrial Production Workers

One of the most important measurements in the practical world of work is the actual number of units turned out on an industrial production line. In the typical pattern, found over and over again by industrial psychologists, work performance goes up sharply in the first ultradian period of the day. Then the curve flattens out a bit, when workers need to take a break. Production then goes up rapidly again until the lunch break at noon. (See Figure 5.)

Efforts to push beyond these natural ultradian phases only lead to inefficiency and error, poor morale, emotional stress, bad judgment, and fatigue-related accidents. In short, a realistic bottom-line attitude recognizes that a company falls into a worsening situation of increasing costs, particularly for employee health services, to pay for the inefficiency that ultradian desynchrony brings to production. These costs can be reduced, while job satisfaction and productivity are increased, when we pay closer heed to our ultradian needs.

White-Collar Workers

The more critical brain power is for a job, the greater the need for ultradian balance. We have seen that the low phase of the ultradian rhythm significantly disrupts intellectual functioning, resulting in longer response time, poor concentration, inefficiency, weakened abstract faculty, forgetfulness, and careless errors.

Paradoxically, people who make their living with their heads are just the ones who tend to work too long. They allow

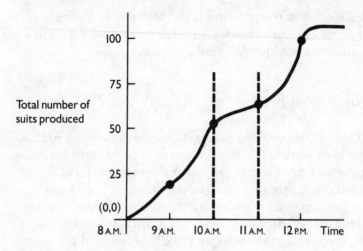

FIGURE 5. *Rates of productivity. This chart shows productivity rates in the garment industry. These rates are typical for industrial production. Notice how the productivity rate flattens out during the normal midmorning break period, delineated by the dashed lines.*

their work demands to overwhelm them into ignoring their mind–body signals, so they end up experiencing the Ultradian Stress Syndrome. Workers in mentally demanding jobs must be encouraged to respect their personal patterns of productivity and recovery.

The goal is to recognize and use those three or four peak periods that come each eight-hour work day. At a recent occupational therapy conference at the University of Southern California, for example, Stephen Hawking, one of the world's most creative astrophysicists, acknowledged that his workday is made up of a series of 90-to-120-minute periods of intense creative work with rest breaks in between.

Creative, effective, and productive people tend to function in sync with their natural rhythms of creative output and take full advantage of the unconscious creativity that their ultradian windows open to them. In the Ultradian Healing Response, we are most able to access the resources of the inner mind. There, we may encounter fresh ideas, directions, and solutions to problems.

For those whose jobs demand high levels of creativity, such as writers, artists, and teachers, observing ultradian recovery breaks is a way to keep in touch with their creative wellsprings. Respecting the ultradian rhythms of activity and rest is one way to avoid the burn-out that afflicts so many creative professionals.

Clerical and Computer Workers

Fifteen million Americans, mostly women, use video display terminals every day. Millions of them come home with sore eyes and pains in their shoulders, back, and neck, and many are now involved in lawsuits and strikes against their employers. Most of this misery could be avoided with ultradian common sense by taking regular breaks.

If your work is repetitive and detail-oriented, take special care to get adequate ultradian restoration. Ultradian fatigue results in concentration problems and errors in spelling, typing, and counting. In fact, public health experts at the University of California at Berkeley recommend that computer users take a 15-minute break every hour or two to refresh themselves and enhance eye recovery. In the ultradian-aware workplace, these breaks should become standard practice.

Telephone Operators

Under the ever-watchful eye of supervisors, telephone operators are expected to handle six hundred to seven hundred calls per day. They must handle an incredible array of subtle but conflicting demands that may even involve emergencies of life and death. These unsung heroes of communication are expected to do all this and still be polite on a 30-second-per-customer basis all day long, with only two 15-minute breaks. That is simply not enough rest for the optimal

performance that is expected of them. Many telephone operators report that they routinely take pain medication before
they come to work and more on the job. They need longer and
more frequent breaks (about thirty minutes) in a quiet room
to enjoy an Ultradian Healing Response.

The Self-Employed

You work for the most demanding, unreasonable, perfec-
tionist slave driver possible: yourself. When the lines between
your enterprise and your personal life are blurry, you can
easily overidentify with work, ignore your mind–body cues,
and fall into the Ultradian Stress Syndrome. When this happens you may disable yourself with psychosomatic problems
such as backaches, headaches, or ulcers.

Consider regular ultradian restoration breaks as a form
of disability insurance, to keep your performance at peak productivity and avoid disrupting your earnings due to a stress-
related physical disability.

Home Workers

The millions of Americans who work at home are among
those most able to apply ultradian principles on a regular
basis. They have the flexibility to work and rejuvenate in accord with their own rhythms, and so maximize their productivity and enjoyment and minimize their stress.

If you work at home, use the Ultradian Healing Response
rather than raiding the refrigerator when you feel the need to
take a break from your work.

Care-Giving Professionals

You cannot provide nurturing care without first nurturing yourself. In the short term, the Ultradian Stress Syndrome

can markedly diminish your effectiveness, impairing your ability to read subtle social cues, reducing your abstract capacities (which help you see patterns, such as gradual changes in a patient's condition or a student's progress), and making you tense and impatient. In the long run, lack of adequate ultradian rejuvenation may be why so many care-givers simply burn out. In every nurturing profession—doctors, nurses, therapists, teachers, counselors—ultradian breaks are vital to keep emotions balanced and interpersonal observations acute.

High-Vigilance and Shift Workers

One of the country's premier sleep researchers, Stanford University's William Dement, estimates that sleepiness and inattention cause more accidents than alcohol, which suggests that ultradian restoration is vitally important for those whose work requires constant vigilance and alertness. Knowing when we are heading into nature's Ultradian Healing Response will help us avoid the slow reactions, inefficient responses, and memory failures that make the ultradian trough especially accident prone.

Particularly those in high-stress jobs in which safety is at stake—such as nuclear-plant operators, air-traffic controllers, surgeons, and heavy-equipment operators—must mind their need for ultradian refreshment. Research shows that pilots and train engineers have more accidents when they don't get adequate recuperative periods. In an ultradian-wise move, the Federal Aviation Administration has now agreed to permit "controlled napping" in the cockpit on certain long-distance routes, while a co-pilot operates the aircraft. (Controlled naps, of course, are simply ultradian breaks.)

A generation of research on fatigue-related accidents shows that the overwhelming majority of vehicular accidents take place in the early morning hours. This is also the time when the most catastrophic accidents of our age have taken place. The atomic plant accidents at Three Mile Island and

Chernobyl and the Union Carbide explosion in Bhopal, India took place during these hours.

Shift workers whose schedules change frequently are at especially high risk for desynchronized ultradian and circadian rhythms. It is very difficult for shift workers to function well, because as soon as they adapt to one set of hours—a process that takes a few weeks—they often change to another schedule. In a recent report, *Catastrophes, Sleep, and Public Policy,* from the Association of Professional Sleep Societies, the following official recommendations were made for shiftwork policy.

MORNING CATASTROPHES The period from 1:00 A.M. to about 8:00 A.M. constitutes a time span in the 24-hour day when human medical and performance catastrophes are far more likely to occur. A secondary and less pronounced zone of vulnerability also occurs in the afternoon from 2:00 to roughly 6:00 P.M. Policy and regulatory agencies in both the public and private sectors should be more aware of the losses society has sustained as a function of diminished capacity during these zones of vulnerability. Increased awareness of these issues, including the fact that they affect all humans, will help prevent some of the more serious consequences of accidents and errors during these periods. The committee urges policymakers in the fields of organized labor, management, and government to consider relevant aspects of sleep physiology that affect performance.

MEDICAL CATASTROPHES Such medical catastrophes as myocardial infarction and strokes are more likely to occur at certain times of the day than at other times. Factors associated with increased risk of medical problems and mortality in the morning after a night's sleep should be further elucidated to more efficiently direct health care resources toward identifying patient populations at risk for such catastrophes and preventing unnecessary morbidity and mortality.

VEHICLE OPERATION Programs should be developed to identify the signs of sleep-related error in vehicle operation and on the job, particularly in industries that have a responsibility to minimize accident and error for the sake of public health and safety, e.g., transportation of hazardous materials, nuclear plants, and so forth.

INADEQUATE SLEEP The committee recognizes that inadequate sleep, even as little as one or two hours less than usual sleep, can greatly exaggerate the tendency for error during the time zones of vulnerability. Moreover, sleep loss combined with a period of stress, such as is faced by working groups before production deadlines or launch deadlines, can lead to personality change and irrational behavior. The committee therefore recommends that industries and services affecting public safety should address the physiological needs of the workers and the safety requirements of society at large. Management should also limit active duty hours for all personnel to assure that adequate time for sleep is obtained between successive periods on duty. These limitations should apply to white-collar and/or decision-making personnel, as well as equipment operators. Such steps must also be coupled with educational programs for workers to foster the physiologically sound use of scheduled rest time.

SHIFTWORK SCHEDULES Attention should be given to the identification of the least adaptive shiftwork schedules and to the implementation of schedules that promote health and safety at minimal expense. The schedules of decision makers and the workload of key personnel should minimize the influence of the biological sleep tendencies that increase the likelihood of human error.

If you have a shift-work job, it is vital that you use the Ultradian Healing Response to get the maximum nonwork restoration to help you withstand the rigors of your shifting work hours.

Professions Involving Negotiation

Many occupations involve negotiation in one form or another. From the yearly discussions of company policy to management–labor mediation to the signing of a new customer, ultradians play a vital, if unsuspected, part.

The Ultradian Stress Syndrome can leave us vulnerable in situations requiring our best negotiating skills, while timely use of the Ultradian Healing Response can enhance our alertness and hone our interpersonal skills. Often negotiations or other meetings become protracted, either through lack of awareness of the costs of fatigue or through a deliberate strategy to make use of the natural fatigue and wearing out of the other side. If you are watching closely, you may see these signs of ultradian stress in yourself as well as in others:

- vulnerability, dependence, and suggestibility
- trouble concentrating, memory problems
- careless errors, overlooking significant details
- irritability and impatience
- misspeaking and lapses of hearing

Obviously, this is not the optimum time to engage in high-stakes, demanding negotiations.

When you feel ultradian-stress cues coming on, heed your mind–body's signals that you need a break. If the others aren't willing to take a break, you can always excuse yourself. Do whatever you can to get away somewhere by yourself for a short ultradian healing period.

Sometimes, prolonged negotiation meetings are forced on disputing parties in the belief that this tactic will ensure a quicker agreement. In typical labor–management impasses, when government mediators are called in, their usual tactic is to force all parties to stay in a closed room together for eight, ten, or even fifteen hours—however long it takes to reach an agreement. While one or both sides might make a concession under these circumstances because of ultradian fatigue, the accompanying resentment at being taken advantage of will color their view of the agreement. The mediators may think they have succeeded, but in actuality they may only have set both parties up for a protracted period of future conflict and further litigation. Feeling itself the loser, each side will find ways to sabotage the agreement later.

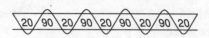

ULTRADIAN TIP:
KEYS TO ULTRADIAN NEGOTIATION

1. Avoid long negotiating sessions. Break them up every hour and a half or so with a 20-minute breather.

2. Avoid negotiations when your mind–body cues indicate you need an Ultradian Healing Response.

3. Monitor yourself and the other participants for cues indicating the onset of the Ultradian Stress Syndrome.

4. Be aware that settlements produced while participants are fatigued and suffering from the Ultradian Stress Syndrome may result in resentment, conflict, and lawsuits.

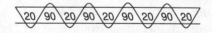

Exploiting ultradian vulnerability, knowingly or unknowingly, is always a poor idea, both ethically and pragmatically. The best strategy is to try to get the meetings to break routinely anytime that a negotiation lasts longer than 90 to 120 minutes. Whether the participants know it or not, this will allow them to get the ultradian restoration they need both to function at their intellectual and emotional best and to optimize the possibility of finding truly creative solutions where everybody wins. It may take longer to reach an accord this way, but it will increase the likelihood that the agreement would be one that all sides could profit from.

ATHLETICS AND ULTRADIANS

On April 23, 1988, the lightweight airplane Daedalus set a world record for human-powered flight, flying 119 kilometers from Crete to the island of Santorini in the Aegean Sea near Greece. Because glucose levels are as important for physical endurance as they are for memory and mind skills, researchers carefully monitored the fast-pedaling pilot's blood glucose level—his mind–body's major fuel—throughout the trip.

Initially the pilot's glucose level went up for the first ultradian period of two hours. It then went down precariously for another two hours before it leveled out slightly higher for the rest of the six-hour trip. This is a clear picture of the limits of human endurance in a struggle for absolute peak performance. It suggests that with suitable breaks, performance is at its highest during our first important ultradian rhythm.

For the sports-minded, this suggests that you must learn how to plan for your peak level of available energy during the first two hours of your performance. During practice periods, athletes need to become skillful in recognizing where they are in their ultradian performance rhythms. Each athlete needs to learn to recognize his or her unique set of mind–body signals of an optimal warm-up phase before a contest begins.

It does no good—and indeed it can be harmful—to over-train to the point where one is straining for higher performance after the initial ultradian rhythm. It is in this period of dwindling energy availability that the athlete can learn bad habits of inefficient performance patterns. This is also the period when poor judgment comes in, along with dwindling enthusiasm and a lessening of the winning spirit. It is a period when accidents and injury are more likely to take place as the athlete becomes tired and careless.

In team sports such as baseball, football, and hockey, the wise coach will learn to recognize the unique pattern of peak performance in each team member as well as the early warning signs when this peak is past. In a good team, the positive relationships between all the members can spark the kind of enthusiasm that entrains optimal performance when the whole team acts in synchrony.

One of the most exciting areas for applying human rhythm research is in the new area of interval training to maximize athletic workouts. At the University of Massachusetts, Dr. Ann Ward compared two groups working out on stationary bikes. Both groups covered the same mileage in 12-minute exercise sessions three days a week, but one group rode steadily for thirty-five minutes while the other rode in intervals— that is to say, in peaks and valleys of effort. Dr. Ward found that the group doing interval training increased oxygen uptake (a cardiovascular fitness measure) by 11 percent over a period of twelve weeks, while the steady-state group remained the same.

In a related study, Dr. Arlette Perry, an exercise physiologist at the University of Miami, compared interval workouts in women's aerobic dancing with steady-pace workouts. Both groups exercised in their 75-to-85-percent target heart range, but one group did aerobics for thirty-five minutes straight while the other interspersed rest periods of brisk walking with 3-to-5-minute intervals of aerobics. At the end of twelve weeks, the interval training group showed an 18-percent improvement in cardiovascular endurance while the steady-state group showed only an 8-percent increase.

At this time, we can only speculate about the reason for improvement in interval-training groups. All evidence, however, is consistent with the ultradian idea that in interval training, athletes learn to facilitate their peaks while they also enjoy deeper recovery during their periods of less intense effort. This type of interval training is illustrated in Figure 6. With this information and the instructions in the following workout plans developed by Elizabeth Kaufmann, you can guide yourself to optimum workouts.

Cycling

- Warm up for five to ten minutes, up to 60 percent of your maximum heart rate.

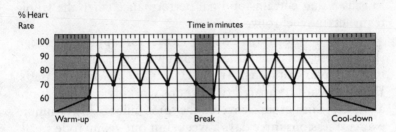

	20	30	40	50	60	Perceived exertion
50%	100	95	90	85	80	Very light
60%	120	114	108	102	96	Fairly light
70%	140	133	126	119	112	Somewhat hard
80%	160	152	144	136	128	Hard
85%	170	162	153	145	136	Very hard
90%	180	171	162	153	144	Very hard

Percent of maximum heart rate

Actual heart rate (beats per minute)

FIGURE 6. *Interval training workouts. The graph illustrates an ultradian athletic interval training workout as expressed by alternating high and low heart rates. The table shows the heart rate in beats per minute for varying age levels. By alternating these peaks and valleys of effort in your workout, you can optimize cardiovascular improvement. (From* American Health, *December 1989.)*

- Ride two minutes at 85 to 90 percent.
- Ride four minutes at a slower pace until heart rate drops to 70 percent
- Repeat this sequence four to six times.
- Take a break; pedal slowly until heart rate drops to 60 percent.
- Do four to six more repetitions at 85 to 90 percent, dropping to 70 percent between reps.
- Cool down for five to ten minutes at 60 percent or lower.

Swimming

- Warm up for five to ten minutes (200 to 500 yards), up to 60 percent of maximum heart rate.

- Swim hard for fifty yards (about forty-five seconds) or one hundred yards (ninety seconds).

- Swim slowly, at your own pace, for 90 or 180 seconds; let heart rate drop to 70 percent.

- Do four to six reps.

- Take a break; stop until heart rate drops to 60 percent.

- Do four to six more reps.

- Cool down for five to ten minutes, at 60 percent or lower.

Running

- Warm up for five to ten minutes, at 60 percent of maximum heart rate.

- Sprint for 45 or 90 seconds at 85 to 90 percent.

- Jog for 90 or 180 seconds; let heart rate drop to 70 percent.

- Do four to six reps.

- Take a break; walk until heart rate drops to 60 percent.

- Do four to six more reps.

- Cool down for five to ten minutes, at 60 percent or lower.

GOING FOR THE GOLD

We are quickly becoming a 24-hour society. We may stay at work till 7:00 P.M., go grocery shopping at 11:00 P.M., watch television till 1:00 A.M., conduct a business transaction at 3:00 A.M. with Europe or Japan, and then go back to the office at 7:00 A.M. for another full day. More and more, people are straining their natural mind–body rhythms to stay one step ahead in a nonstop world. But as Dr. William Dement, director of Stanford University's sleep research center, remarked in a *Time* magazine cover story "Drowsy America": "Most Americans no longer know what it feels like to be fully alert. They go through the day in a sort of twilight zone; the eyes may be wide open, but the brain is partly shut down."

The Ultradian Healing Response offers us a much-needed solution to a fast-paced world. Whatever your profession, your ambition, or your ability, if you begin to make an ultradian break—or several breaks—a regular part of your daily agenda, you will experience renewed energy, creativity, and enjoyment in all your activities. Winning your gold medal could be only twenty minutes away!

7

ULTRADIANS AND DIET, WEIGHT CONTROL, AND ADDICTIONS

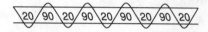

Our society has not yet made its peace with the basic biological reality of our need to eat every 90 to 120 minutes. In this chapter, we will apply what we know of ultradian rhythms to appetite regulation, weight loss and maintenance, and healthier eating patterns in general. We will also explore how an ultradian awareness can assist in breaking various addictions and dependencies from smoking to alcohol and drugs.

APPETITE REGULATION THE ULTRADIAN WAY

Americans will spend more than 35 billion dollars this year on diet-related products and services, but most popular diets and quick weight-loss schemes are written in complete ignorance of the body's natural ultradian hunger rhythms. It is a biological fact that every 90 to 120 minutes, the stomach undergoes a rhythmic series of contractions—a hunger pang. This means that the traditional recommendations of three square meals a day with snacks discouraged is actually out of sync with our underlying ultradian needs. If we heeded our ultradian rhythms, we would eat not three times each day, but six.

The fact is, when we become hungry, we are usually responding to a rhythm established when our humanoid ancestors foraged in the primeval forests eons ago, sustaining themselves with small but frequent meals. These hunger rhythms come every ninety minutes or so because they are paced in part by the brain's appetite-control center which lies close to the brain centers of the hypothalamus, which play a role in maintaining our ultradian rhythms.

Many studies have also shown that humans exhibit a pronounced oral need—to drink, smoke, or nibble—on a 90-minute schedule. Research from Mount Sinai Hospital in New York found that volunteers, left on thir own in an environment without any time cues and told to help themselves to food, drink, or cigarettes whenever they felt like it, did so on a regular schedule—at a mean interval of ninety-six minutes.

In our modern culture, however, we regularly overeat at least three times a day and them unwittingly deprive ourselves of vitally needed sustenance at least three other times. For every meal we eat, we have actually missed one meal that our body wants. By skipping our ultradian calls for sustenance every few hours, we incur significant energy deficits and become much hungrier than we should be. Then when we finally do sit down to eat, having ignored our natural ultradian cues for hunger, we not only tend to eat far more than we need but also the wrong things. We eat much more sugar, salt, and fat and far less healthy protein and complex carbohydrates than we should. Ultimately, this habit is what leads to weight gain and increased cholesterol levels and taxes our body's digestive process.

In contrast, ultradian-aware eating promotes positive changes in your health and your waistline. Ultradian-sensitive eating helps you in the following ways.

It keeps your weight stable or reduces it. By developing sensitivity to ultradian cues, you become more aware of your body–mind's hunger signals. That awareness helps you to avoid ravenous hunger and overwhelming food cravings that cause you to overeat or fall off diets and to recognize the cues when you are full.

You eat healthy food in appropriate quantities. By eating the ultradian way you will actually eat better, more healthful, food. When we fall into the state of nutritional desperation that comes with ignoring our ultradian eating cues, we can lose our good judgment and settle for what is available—too often, junk food. But when we eat small quantities on a regular ultradian schedule, we never get to that overhungry state.

It heightens your overall energy and productivity. Eating on our natural ultradian rhythm also helps spare us from the wide swings of alertness and fatigue that can occur during the day when we overload the digestive system by eating too many calories in a single large meal. Eating smaller, nutritious meals or snacks in tune with our ultradian cues helps to stabilize blood-sugar levels, which in turn optimizes memory, learning, and performance. The ultradian rhythm approach to eating embodies many of the same principles physicians have long used to treat hypoglycemic and diabetic patients whose unstable blood-sugar levels cause a variety of associated mind–body illnesses.

Ultradian eating is compatible with any special or restricted diet you may observe and supports most medically based diets. If you have to watch sodium intake or fats or are a vegetarian, you can still use the ultradian approach to eating. Diets recommended by the American Diabetes Association, the American Heart Association, the American Dietetic Association, and Weight Watchers are all compatible with such an approach.

This small-portion, frequent-meal eating plan is also recommended by the American Dietetic Association for young children, as well as for the elderly. Toddlers and preschoolers need frequent nourishment to supply all the nutrients they need to grow and develop, and seniors digest food better and function with more adequate energy levels throughout the day when they eat several mini-meals.

Growing Pains

Let's look more closely at the biological rationale for ultradian-aware eating. When we eat a large meal, particularly if it is loaded with sugars and fats, the pancreas releases a quantity of insulin into the bloodstream. This messenger molecule tells the cells of the body to metabolize, that is, to burn the sugars or store them for future use.

It usually takes one ultradian period, from 90 to 120 minutes, for the blood-sugar and insulin levels to peak and then stabilize before another hunger rhythm is set in motion. Researchers have found that the peak in insulin follows the glucose peak by about twenty minutes. This probably accounts for our need to take a break for about twenty minutes after we eat a meal, as the mind–body needs its resources to assimilate food energy.

Unfortunately, most of us tend to eat large meals or snacks overloaded with refined carbohydrates and simple sugars. These burn in a flash and call for a large secretion of insulin to deal with the excess calories. This results in a rapid crash in blood-sugar levels and a correspondingly quicker call for more blood glucose, and so we eat more. We may even get caught in a yo-yoing cycle of sugar and carbohydrate cravings and crashes, which can lead to binge eating and extreme weight gain.

Recent research confirms these dramatic mind–body connections between appetite, food cravings, and the insulin–blood–sugar rhythm. Even the sight and smell of tempting food can trigger the release of insulin for some people, so that even if they don't eat the food they see, the mind affects the release of insulin, which tends to sweep up whatever sugars are flowing through the bloodstream and pull them into cells for fat storage. Some researchers propose that even the thought of tempting food may trigger weight gain. (Fortunately, the reverse may also be true. An athlete who uses imagery to rehearse a sports performance within the mind's eye may actually set in motion the messenger molecules that will help fats break down to be metabolized into energy and weight reduction. This implies that thinking thin could actually work.)

In any event, consider the following typical scenario: you are seated at a restaurant, having gone without food for several hours. Because your blood sugar is low, the appetite center in the brain has already been signaling a need for food for too long. As you sit down, the eating cues—the sight and smell of food, the descriptions on the menu—further entrain your ultradian rhythms into a higher pitch of hunger.

As you peruse the menu, the cerebral cortex of your brain transmits a series of ideas ("Gosh, I'm starved," or "Hmm, fresh swordfish with butter sauce") through the mind-brain message centers of the limbic-hypothalamic system. There, the cognitive messages from the higher cortex are turned into rhythmic flows of messenger molecules that travel to the stomach and trigger contractions, which you feel as rumbles or hunger pangs. You are hungry and primed to eat.

As soon as you sit down, the waiter asks, "Would you like a drink?" You respond affirmatively. Alcohol is a stopgap measure, a quickly absorbed source of empty calories. You need nutritious calories, not the empty calories of alcohol, but you consume a drink before your meal.

Finally you order. Still operating in semistarvation mode, craving calories, your tendency is to order a lot of the wrong things—foods rich in fat, heavy dishes—anything to get you out of the food-deficit state your brain senses. Meanwhile, while you wait, you reach for the bread or rolls, craving carbohydrates to stem your younger. You might also slather them with butter, adding calories from fat.

Soon, the primarily empty calories you have consumed take the edge off the intense caloric craving from your frustrated ultradian rhythms. After an appetizer, bread, and drinks, your body may already have all the calories it needs. But satiety doesn't register in your appetite centers yet, because it takes about twenty minutes from when you start eating until your intestinal tract releases the messenger molecule cholecystokinin (CCK) to signal the brain that you are now eating or have eaten enough.

Unfortunately, the CCK messenger may still not have arrived at the brain when the main course arrives. You continue to eat, much faster than messenger molecules can convey their message that you have had enough. We have all asked ourselves at some time or other, as heaping dinner plates are brought to the table, "How will I ever eat all this?" But because the signaling molecules have not yet gotten their message through, we eat what is in front of us, whether we need it or even want it. Out of step with our ultradian hunger cues, it is easy to overindulge—and get fat.

THE ULTRADIAN WAY TO HEALTHIER EATING

There is a more enlightened option: learning how to eat with an awareness of our mind–body ultradian cues and rhythms. The cornerstone of ultradian nutrition is the human body's built-in need to eat every 90 to 120 minutes. Following are the six related and mutually supporting principles that make up the ultradian approach to food intake.

1. Know and respect your ultradian mind–body cues for hunger. Pay attention to your natural hunger pangs every 90 to 120 minutes. Often we experience these as oral cravings, or thoughts and fantasies about food.

2. When your ultradian cues call, eat something! Don't hold yourself back because it is not mealtime. Respect your natural mind–body rhythms, and eat lighter, healthier meals five or six times a day. Mealtimes then will not become artificial and desperate attempts to eat yourself out of a self-imposed state of starvation.

3. Eat small amounts of complex foods as your ultradian cues signal you. Fresh fruits and vegetables contain the complex carbohydrates, fiber, vitamins, and minerals in nutritious combinations that are ultimately more satisfying than sugar and simple carbohydrates because they release their nutrients and calories in a slower fashion to help you avoid the yo-yoing binge syndrome.

4. Decide in advance what and how you will eat. Don't just start eating and continue until you feel full. You will be amazed at how easily telling yourself what you need and what will be satisfying becomes a self-fulfilling prophecy.

5. Eat your allotted amount. If you are still hungry, relax into a comfortable Ultradian Healing Response. That allows sufficient times for the messengers and blood-sugar levels regulating hunger to signal your brain appetite center that you have eaten enough. Since you now feel full, there is no further temptation to eat calories you don't need. Eating a light meal or snack of 100 to 200 calories before your break, in fact, works in harmony with the purpose of twenty minutes of rest, since food entrains your natural Ultradian Healing Response.

6. Divide your total daily calorie requirement into six installments. Don't just add in-between-meal snacks to your three normal meals—that will only increase your total daily calorie intake and defeat the purpose of the ultradian approach.

A recent scientific study supports the fact that smaller

meals eaten at greater frequency throughout the day can also facilitate cholesterol control. A dozen researchers, under the leadership of Dr. David Jenkins in Toronto, placed normal males on two identical diets, but one group ate the food in three meals per day while the other ate the same total amount in a series of seventeen hourly snacks.

The research indicated that the stabilization of the glucose–insulin rhythms is fundamental to controlling cholesterol: the levels of low-density lipids (LDL, so-called bad cholesterol) were 13.5 percent lower among the group that ate small amounts hourly. Their total cholesterol count, a combination of LDL and HDL (high-density lipids, so-called good cholesterol) declined 8.5 percent. Total cholesterol fell from an average of 204 to 172 during the two-week period of the study. It seems that the insulin released by the pancreas can also stimulate an enzyme in the liver to produce cholesterol, which floods the bloodstream in excessive amounts. This phenomenal improvement with ultradian hourly eating was achieved with a diet that contained 33 percent fat, although current medical recommendations in the United States are for no more than 30 percent dietary fat.

ADVICE TO OVEREATERS

There are many ways knowledge of ultradian rhythms can help those who have special trouble balancing food intake. In clinical practice, I have recognized four classic types of overeaters who can be helped with the ultradian approach. They are profiled below together with the ultradian solution for each. Most people fall into one of these categories at some time in their lives. You have a problem only if you are chronically stuck in one or more patterns.

Stress overeater. You overeat and oversnack at any time of the day in direct response to the stresses of everyday life.
The Ultradian Solution. Recognize your stress limits and

learn how to say no before you reach them. Then use the Ultradian Healing Response to break the the stress syndrome and gain some perspective on those situations you need to cope with more creatively.

Fatigue overeater. In a futile effort to overcome stress and fatigue, you snack almost continually after 3:00 or 4:00 P.M., even after a full meal, and continue until bedtime.

The Ultradian Solution. Pace yourself better throughout the day with two or three ultradian healing periods and a mid-afternoon nap to cut back on fatigue buildup. Experiment with healthful snacks of 200 to 300 calories of complex carbohydrates before your ultradian break so that the food energy can be assimilated in an ideal manner for fatigue reduction and energy restoration.

Addictive overeater. You are a cyclic overeater or drinker who constantly consumes addictive substances such as caffeine (coffee, tea, chocolate, or cola drinks) or alcohol (beer, wine, or hard liquor). You may also use calories—especially sugars and fats—for their mood-altering effects in an effort to stave off depression.

The Ultradian Solution. Study the ultradian pattern of your addiction. How long is it between the time you overindulge and the time when you begin to feel you need another fix? Use the Ultradian Healing Response before or just as soon as you recognize your withdrawal craving beginning. This maximizes your mind–body's capacity to heal the withdrawal symptoms with natural beta-endorphins and other messenger molecules that make you feel comfortable and rejuvenated.

Escapist overeater. You often eat alone in an effort to escape unpleasant realities you do not know how to cope with.

The Ultradian Solution. Here the psychological element in the Ultradian Healing Response comes into play. Use the time when you would use eating as an escape to make an inventory of your life and what it is you really want from food.

Pose questions to your inner mind that may be answered during or soon after the Ultradian Healing Response. Ask yourself for fresh ideas in dealing with your problems. Let the deeper levels of your inner mind help you to find the answers.

Here is an example of how one of my clients used the ultradian diet and the Ultradian Healing Response to lose more than thirty pounds of excess weight he had had most of his adult life. This patient, a sixty-seven-year-old lawyer, complained that he always ate more than he really wanted. After a year of rather unsuccessful conventional psychotherapeutic approaches to diet control (and a lifetime of unsuccessful dieting by all known methods), he began eating six small meals, each containing 200 to 300 well-balanced calories, spaced throughout the day to coincide with his natural Ultradian Healing Response.

The lawyer learned to use the ultradian healing periods after these meals for what he called deep meditations on his destructive eating patterns. During these breaks, he spontaneously received insights into the early-life sources of his hunger in a series of remarkable flashbacks wherein he recalled his mother forcing him to eat and insisting that he finish everything on his plate. His insights helped him to control his finish-it-all-up compulsion. A year after therapy, he reported that he continued to control his weight in a satisfactory manner.

What is most noteworthy about this case is that the weight-control program was successful only after the patient introduced a number of ultradian healing periods throughout the day when he was able to explore deeply the source of his hunger-related behaviors. Like many people with weight-control problems who are unable to understand the psychological causes of their overeating, he found the Ultradian Healing Response to be significant in helping him establish a safe time and place for the resolution of deep-seated issues. The security of an ultradian break several times a day, with appropriate caloric intake, may provide optimal conditions for dealing with many such psychological issues.

ADDITIONAL BODY-RHYTHM FACTORS IN WEIGHT CONTROL

The interconnectedness of our ultradian rhythms with our circadian and infradian rhythms is complex. Following are some additional considerations about our daily, monthly, and seasonal rhythms that influence our eating habits and our ability to maintain a healthy weight.

Daily Rhythms and Weight Control

Current research appears to support the view that circadian rhythms also play an important role in the control of weight. This research suggests that the weight gain a calorie causes depends upon the time of day when it is consumed and that calories taken earlier in the day cause less weight gain and lead to better health.

One well-conducted study confirming the circadian weight connection was carried out by Dr. Bellisle and reported in the journal *Appetite* in 1988. Children ranging in age from seven to twelve years were classified into the five weight categories of lean, slim, average, fat, and obese on the basis of a weight/height index. Although all the children ate roughly the same number of calories each day, distribution of caloric intake throughout the day varied. The researchers reported, "[The] obese and fat children ate less at breakfast and more at dinner than their leaner peers. The traditionally larger meals (lunch and dinner) represented higher proportions of daily intake in [the] fat and obese children: the energy value of breakfast and afternoon snacks was inversely related to corpulence." The researchers concluded that "the results suggest a possible contribution of disturbed metabolic and/or behavioral daily cycles in the development of overweight. This hypothesis, which should be investigated further, suggests prevention strategies."

Other clinicians, with extensive experience counseling people in weight control, also confirm that overeating at night is a typical pattern in overweight people. A circadian approach to this problem is the introduction of appropriate activity and social support during the late-afternoon and evening hours.

For example, Jan, a young woman I worked with, found that when she took an acting class at her local university extension two evenings a week, she was able to displace her need for at least 2,000 calories with more meaningful activity that enhanced her self-image and social skills. She learned to gain sustenance from the supportive class and the new friends she made in rehearsal sessions several other times a week. Over the period of one school semester she found herself naturally within her ideal weight range with hardly a thought of dieting.

A good example of the benefits that can come from attending to circadian eating patterns coupled with using the Ultradian Healing Response comes from Canadian therapist Rosemary Liburd. The following is an excerpt from the ultradian diary of Liburd's client Debra, who was struggling with chronic weight gain.

> I used to find myself feeling very tired around 4:00 or 5:00 P.M. I would get home after a long day and my pattern was to make myself something to eat. I would come in the door and head straight to the refrigerator, telling myself "I'll just have one small snack." But it rarely stopped there. Frequently, I would start to eat and just continue for the rest of the afternoon and evening.

Such uncontrolled eating was not typical of Debra earlier in the day, so she felt it was a reaction to the stressful emotional demands of her workday. Discussion revealed that using food to cope with anxiety was a lifelong pattern for Debra, starting with feeding schedules as an infant, all the way through college and into adulthood. The therapist prescribed regular periods of ultradian healing to reduce the tension that was driving Debra into the arms of her refrigerator. Six months later, the therapist found herself facing a

Debra who was about twenty pounds lighter and very excited. Debra's diary tells the story:

> I do my ultradian refreshers about twice a day, and have for the last six months. When I feel my stress level rising, or my energy dropping, I use ultradian recuperation for energy. It is particularly helpful at the end of the morning's appointments, when my energy is low and I need a boost.

The most dramatic effect, Debra explains, comes when she takes an ultradian break in the late afternoon.

> At about 4:00 or 5:00, when I get home, instead of heading straight for a snack, I treat myself to an ultradian break. I ask my subconscious if it is ready to let me take a deep and relaxing and complete ultradian rest. Often, I use the nasal-head shift to facilitate ultradian healing.
>
> I feel much more in control after using ultradians. It has completely diminished my need to overeat. Now I find I can wait to eat supper, I don't need to eat all night long, and I stay awake longer because my energy is higher. I definitely feel that taking ultradian breaks made a huge difference.

If you are stuck in a destructive embrace with food, the Ultradian Healing Response can give you the restoration and rejuvenation necessary to make the changes you need to bring your relationship with food back into balance.

Spend two weeks eating the ultradian way: sparingly but often, whenever your cues beckon. It will take some getting used to, for it is not easy to break lifelong eating patterns, and our society is not set up to encourage the eating of smaller meals six times a day. But as you make this change, you will find yourself feeling stronger, less emotionally and physically volatile, and more alert. Most of all, it will help you avoid the destructive semistarvation syndrome that creates too much weight and too little health. Beginning with your next meal in ninety minutes or so, you can start nourishing yourself in cooperation, not in competition, with your body—by eating the ultradian way.

Monthly Rhythms and Weight Control

Weight also varies in infradian rhythms for both men and women, although it is more obvious in women. The mind–body reasons for this have recently become clearer as we have learned more about the typical rhythms in the timing of the hormonal messenger molecules of the monthly menstrual cycle.

At least three messenger molecules are intimately involved in the relationship between appetite and a woman's monthly menstrual rhythm: estrogen, progesterone, and insulin. Dr. Henrietta Spencer of Beverly Hills has explored the theory of how these hormones interact during pubertal development, the monthly cycle, and pregnancy. Following is a summary of her ideas:

Estrogen. It may be that women are literally shaped by their sex hormones, as estrogen, menstruation, and the storage and location of body fat are all linked. Estrogen, produced primarily in the ovaries, initiates a girl's pubertal development. Breasts develop, pelvis bones grow and widen, and total body fat increases on hips, rear, and thighs. Estrogen feeds the adipose (fat) cells in these areas by encouraging them to produce more of an enzyme, lipoprotein lipose (LPL). The high presence of LPL in turn pulls fat from the bloodstream into the adipose cells.

Women can control estrogen levels to some extent through reducing fats in their daily diet and eating greater amounts of high-fiber foods. Fiber in the diet may reduce estrogen levels by binding to estrogen in the intestines and eliminating it from the body through the bowel.

Progesterone. The role of progestrone in the menstrual cycle and pregnancy suggests that it is also related to weight gain. The insulin connection operates in both men and women but apparently is a greater issue for women. When progesterone levels are high, the cell receptors tend to bind insulin, which in turn promotes the accumulation of fat storage.

During pregnancy progesterone production goes up and remains high for nine months, when food temptations are at their peak. In effect, nature is trying to tell the mother to eat for two. Even when a woman is not pregnant, however, there are monthly peaks in progesterone levels about midway through the menstrual cycle. At these times many women tend to binge on food, especially to have cravings for carbohydrates.   ·

One way women can deal with this appetite for carbohydrates is to permit themselves a realistic increase in complex carbohydrates during the two weeks before their period. It is possible to avoid yo-yo binging on sugar and simple carbohydrates by allowing about 150 extra complex carbohydrate calories a day during this period. Pregnant women can take in about twice that amount every day.

Insulin. There are a number of common-sense approaches to dealing with the insulin factor in weight control. Avoid sugar and simple carbohydrates, such as sweets, ice cream, and cake, which tend to trigger excessive amounts of insulin into the bloodstream. Reduce the size of meals, eating sensibly about six times a day instead of consuming three large meals. Beware of caffeine-containing drinks such as coffee, tea, chocolate, and cola, since caffeine releases stored sugars from the liver into the bloodstream and could set off a yo-yoing binge.

An example of how the craving for simple sugars can be controlled with an ultradian approach was presented by Arleen Rainis, a psychotherapist in North Carolina.

A 37-year-old client contacted me requesting help with her "addiction for sugar." She routinely binged on sugar and sweets and had a particular weakness for the icing on cakes. I saw the client a total of seven times over a two-month period, and taught her to use the Ultradian Healing Response four to six times daily. She was able to do only one to two 20-minute ultradian breaks daily. However, she did follow the directions given for the Ultradian Healing Response.

The client reports that she has not eaten any sugar for the past four and a half months. During this period, she has been to three birthday parties and has been exposed to the type of cake she formerly found irresistible. She ate none of it. When in a social situation she is offered a piece of pie with coffee, she refuses, stating: "I don't do pie!" The most significant change she reports is the total lack of physical craving for sugar. She is still aware of her psychological/emotional desire for it, but can control that when she is able to replace it with the comfort of an Ultradian Healing Response.

She describes herself as being "inner-motivated," which is a new experience for her. When asked if it was difficult to find time for the ultradian breaks each day, she laughingly replied, "Are you kidding? It's a piece of cake!"

While the just-say-no approach is obviously an important factor in any weight-control diet, the point of such testimony is that the comfort of the Ultradian Healing Response can be used as a healthy reward replacing the illusion of well-being brought on by a sugar rush.

Seasonal Rhythms and Weight Control

Further evidence for the many connections between mind–body rhythms on many levels is the recent research on seasonal affective disorder (SAD). With the reduction in the amount of daylight during the winter months, some animals consume vast quantities of starches that lead to fat storage and weight gain in preparation for hibernation. In the same ways, a tendency toward sedentary habits and emotional depression is characteristic of some people during the winter months, particularly those suffering from SAD.

Although research shows that light therapy and exercise can help to lessen both the tendency for weight gain and depression, Dr. Norman Rosenthal and his colleagues at the National Institute of Mental Health found that carbohydrate-rich meals can energize SAD patients (although the same meals usually make normal people feel sedated and sleepy). Since depression with its low-energy feeling is characteristic of SAD patients, he suggests that they seek out carbohydrate-rich foods to increase their energy and metabolism.

Apart from the unique program of light enhancement early in the day, many of the solutions proposed by Rosenthal's group are already familiar to us: eating complex rather than simple carbohydrates, increasing fiber in the diet, reducing stress, increasing exercise, making use of psychotherapy and counseling to resolve emotional issues, and continually exploring new activities that can foster an increased sense of purpose.

ULTRADIAN APPROACHES TO ADDICTIONS

Our discussion above of weight control raises an important and related topic: addictions. In recent years we have recognized a growing proliferation of addictive behaviors. Gambling, working, exercising, sex, and even computer hacking have all been described as addictive behavior.

While the psychological and sociological factors behind addictive behaviors are complex and will vary from person to person, everything we have learned about the Ultradian Stress Syndrome suggests that binge behavior of any sort signals an addictive behavior when it interferes with our normal ultradian and circadian rhythms. The substances of abuse in all of these behavioral addictions are our own natural mind–body messenger molecules poured out to excess. When we chronically override our normal ultradian–circadian rest periods, we become addicted to an emotional high from our own stress-released hormonal messenger molecules.

Much of the research on addiction is so new that it has not yet been translated into practical treatments. Many therapists familiar with the Ultradian Healing Response, however, are beginning to explore how this approach may be applied. Since we know that addictions are linked with disruptions of our natural ultradian rhythms, these therapists are recommending ultradian approaches as a valuable tool for breaking the stress–addiction cycle.

The Ultradian Healing Response can work in three ways to help us avoid and overcome addictions. First, ultradian breaks sensitize us to our natural mind–body signals for a period of rest and recovery, making us less likely to drive ourselves into the Ultradian Stress Syndrome that sets the stage for substance abuse. Second, they provide an easy method to help recovering abusers take care of themselves so that everyday stresses do not build up to the point at which they are tempted to relapse. Third, consistent use of the Ultradian Healing Response can facilitate recovery from the emotional dysphoria (depression) and anhedonia (lack of pleasure) during the withdrawal period and afterwards.

If you feel you are addicted, whether to nicotine, alcohol, drugs, gambling, or any other substance or habit, consider the following ultradian tips for recovery:

1. Feeling the desire for a drug—whether a cup of coffee, a stiff drink, a beer, a relaxing cigarette, or a hit of cocaine—is a prime cue that you are beginning to experience the Ultradian Stress Syndrome.

2. The best thing you can do at that moment is to take a breather to get in touch with yourself.

3. Recognize that you are under stress and need release and recovery. Instead of indulging in your usual addiction, see this as an opportunity to heal whatever tension you might otherwise have resolved with substance abuse.

4. Sit or lie down and allow your natural Ultradian Healing Response to occur.

It is always better to reach for the comfort of an Ultradian Healing Response than for an addictive substance. The Ultradian Healing Response can facilitate the release of the natural messenger molecules that your mind–body is craving. Your substance of abuse was only a dangerous substitute for what nature can give you free, whenever you heed your ultradian call.

8

THE ULTRADIAN FAMILY

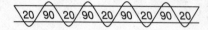

Every family lives by rhythms. Many of these rhythms are seasonal, such as religious observances, holiday preparations, summer vacations, and the quiet of indoor activities in winter. Families also have daily cycles—waking and sleeping, the work and school day, and relaxing together in the evening. Many family rhythms are ultradian: we tend to spend an hour or two doing chores, playing, doing homework, or watching television. In addition, our families often span several generations, each of which has its own age-specific rhythms: the fast feeding/sleeping rhythm of the newborn, the play and school rhythms of older children, the work and rest cycles of mother and father, and the more leisurely pace of grandparents.

Although we speak of a family unit, it is more accurate to say that we are a pride of interacting individuals, each moving in his or her own rhythmic patterns, each moving in and out of synchrony with the family group. Our family dynamics—how we get along—reflect a complex mandala of these individual rhythms and the changes of consciousness and behavior associated with them. Unaware of the rhythmic changes going on in us, we may we find ourselves out of sympathetic harmony with family members.

When families fall out of synchrony, everyone feels irritable, overwhelmed, put upon, disconnected, and isolated. When such desynchrony becomes chronic, the fabric of the family can be rent and familial love and support become submerged in a maelstrom of stressful emotions.

Until now, there hasn't been much awareness of these seasonal, daily, and ultradian rhythms as a symphony that enables families to function harmoniously together or fall into discord. By applying our currently developing knowledge of our natural family rhythms, it is possible to recognize and cope with many common family dynamics and to:

- improve bonding between infants, children, and parents
- foster a calmer, more loving home environment
- help teens manage the important life changes they are experiencing
- enhance senior living

In this chapter, we will explore these and related issues. The two ultradian links to family harmony can be summarized as follows:

- *Sharing ultradian synchrony with family members can enhance familial unity and harmony.* The better we respect and synchronize with the ultradian rhythms of those we live with, the more harmonious and stable our home environment becomes.
- *Reducing each person's ultradian stress is an important factor in healing the dysfunctional family.* Just as ultradian relaxation helps restore us to perform better at work, it helps us be better and more sensitive mothers, fathers, and family members.

NEW FAMILY RHYTHMS

For beginning families—those who are expecting or raising infants—understanding the ultradian basis of family dynamics and relationships can promote healthy, happy, and harmonious times together. In this section, we will examine:

- ultradians in the unborn
- ultradians and nursing mothers
- ultradians and parent–infant bonding

Ultradians in the Pre-Born

In the early stages of pregnancy, it is believed that mother and baby seem to keep roughly the same ultradian schedule. Because the fetus is a part of the mother's body, sharing many messenger molecules and nutrients, it is affected by the same sweeping changes that move throughout her body on the 90-to-120-minute ultradian schedule.

Starting at about the second trimester of pregnancy, however, fetuses develop their own distinct rhythms in sleeping, alertness, heart rate, brain waves, and body movement. As early as twenty-three weeks, the developing fetus shows a clear REM ultradian rhythm and a distinct ultradian rhythm in heart rate. Mothers are obviously aware of these rhythms when they feel the shifts, moves, and kicks within; these are probably reflections of the fetus's ultradian peak activity period, which may or may not coincide with the mother's own peak activity periods.

At birth an infant's many ultradian rhythms run at a fast pace, approximately every 40 to 60 minutes or so. By about eight months of age, most of the baby's bodily systems—urine output, temperature, pulse rate, blood chemistry, and even brain function—settle into the approximately 90-to-120-minute rhythm they will keep throughout life. Many researchers now believe that these 90-to-120-minute ultradians are the basic rhythms of which our longer daily (circadian) and seasonal (infradian) rhythms are composed. By learning how to recognize these ultradian rhythms, we can optimize many aspects of family life, beginning with pregnancy.

During pregnancy it is doubly important to use the Ultradian Healing Response to counter any signs of the Ultradian

Stress Syndrome, because you are timing for two. You need extra recuperation because of the extra stress the fetus puts on your body. This is especially true because during pregnancy stress hormones such as cortisol and epinephrine cross the placenta and can adversely affect fetal development. Now is the time you most need to heed your mind–body cues for ultradian restoration. Not only is your personal well-being at stake, but also that of the baby developing within.

The following signs indicate that it is time for pregnant women to heed their ultradian needs:

- increasing needs for sleep, rest, and naps
- changing rhythms of eating, digestion, and urination
- changing personality and interest patterns
- altered sensory acuity, body blance, and activity level

If you are pregnant, these signals are telling you that you need to seek natural restoration through the Ultradian Healing Response.

Arlene Rainis reports how ultradian restoration helped one woman, a 36-year-old musician, cope with the physical and emotional demands of pregnancy:

> The client learned to use the Ultradian Healing Response to reduce deep fatigue and mood swings associated with the hormonal changes of pregnancy, as well as to increase positive perspectives on life in general. The client reported: "I was amazed at how simple it was. I have no doubt that all the positive changes came from that."

Ideally, the Ultradian Healing Response can also be a valuable tool in helping pregnant women addicted to alcohol and other drugs. It is estimated that fetal alcohol syndrome (FAS) is responsible for 50,000 children being born each year with some form of impairment or birth defect due to maternal drinking. Because most of the alcohol a pregnant mother drinks ends up passing through her placenta and is distributed in the amniotic fluid surrounding the embryonic child, the fetus is directly affected. Fortunately, in the Ultradian Healing Response nature has given expectant mothers a drug free, naturally safe tool to eliminate or reduce stress and help keep babies healthy.

Ultradians and Nursing Mothers

The warmth of a nursing mother's body and her touch are strong ultradian entrainers that put the mother and her child into a natural state of ultradian synchrony. In fact, it takes about ten to twenty minutes to nurse a child—the length of one natural Ultradian Healing Response.

Recent research suggests that ultradian relaxation can also aid the nursing mother. Doctors from the University of New Mexico studied a group of mothers of premature babies in neonatal intensive care. These mothers were having trouble providing natural breastmilk because of the anxiety and fatigue surrounding the births. One group of mothers took a 20-minute break, during which they listened to a relaxing audio tape. These mothers increased their milk production by 63 percent over those who did not.

California psychologist Brian Lippincott has reported one case in which the Ultradian Healing Response helped facilitate milk production in a patient experiencing extreme anxiety about nursing:

Lucy was a 21-year-old patient in marriage counseling when her first child was born. Shortly after the birth she phoned me one night to report severe anxiety because she could not breast-feed her daughter. She explained that she would lie down while facing her daughter and attempt to breast-feed her, but the milk would not come. Then the baby would cry and a vicious cycle of guilt and anxiety would develop.

Prior to the call, both Lucy and her husband, Jack, had been taught the basics of ultradian healing, including the brain-breath shift technique. I had initially suggested it to them as a strategic intervention to stop their angry escalation during arguments.

One the phone I asked Lucy to check for nostril dominance, and she reported that the right nostril was dominant (open). She also reported that she had been lying on her left side trying to sleep and feed the baby. I instructed Lucy to lie down on her right side and take a 20-minute ultradian break. Then her husband was to bring her the baby to feed while she was still lying on the right side. The next morning, Lucy reported that this intervention with the Ultradian Healing Response had indeed helped her milk to resume flowing.

While this clinical anecdote is obviously not enough to prove the connection between brain dominance and breast-feeding, it portends a new area of research that we might explore to help new mothers who have difficulty nursing their infants.

Deepening the Parent–Infant Bond

Why do some young mothers and fathers seem to sail through the early months of their baby's life, while others become exhausted, irritable, and stressed? And why, from the very earliest age, is one infant placid, obliging, and sweet-tempered and another colicky, frustrating, and difficult? Lacking an obvious explanation, most parents would shrug and attribute such differences to personality. However, in such cases, the underlying issue may be the synchrony or de-synchrony of ultradian rhythms between parents and child.

For example, consider a baby who is on a generally consistent waking-and-feeding rhythm. In such a case, the mother and father can more easily synchronize the infant's feeding

schedule with their own ultradian cycles. Properly synchronized, the baby's need for nighttime feedings especially would
come at the same point that the parents' 90-minute REM
dream cycles naturally bring them closer to waking consciousness. The father and mother would lose porportionately
less of their vitally need deep, restorative sleep and would
awaken more rested, less stressed, and better able to provide
their infant with loving, nurturing care.

On the other hand, a child on a seemingly random
feeding-and-waking routine may offer no clear pattern for father or mother to synchronize with. In such cases, the adults'
nighttime sleep cycles are fractured, their deep sleep constantly interrupted, and they fall into a descending spiral of
stress and exhaustion. Having several children close in age,
each going through the process of synchronizing its own ultradian rhythms with those of other family members, can be
particularly taxing.

Although it is impossible to predict what your baby's
feeding patterns will be, bear in mind the basic ultradian prin-
ciple: in the beginning, the mother and father should strive to
get in synchrony with the ultradian rhythms of the baby. You
can achieve this by giving the infant cues and signals—
rocking, holding, feeding, playing music, or turning down the
lights—to help entrain him or her to a schedule that is closer
to yours. You connect by getting into synchrony with the
child, then you modulate his or her rhythmic behaviors by entraining them to your own. This means, however, that you
need to learn your baby's rhythms before you can entrain him
or her to your own.

For example, when it comes to feeding, do not start by
imposing a rigid feeding schedule, but instead attune yourself
to recognizing your baby's natural ultradian cues and
rhythms.

Then, little by little, entrain all your ultradian rhythms to
harmonize. By being sensitive to the rhythmic nature of your
baby's early months, you may establish the foundation for a
lifetime of family togetherness.

ULTRADIANS AND
THE ESTABLISHED FAMILY

The social functioning of the established family is a rich tapestry of intermeshing ultradian rhythms. Older children are more autonomous individuals, bringing their own schedules and rhythms to the family symphony. At this stage, the rhythms of the family may face desynchrony and stress as members leave and return from work or school at different times. Family activities such as meals and chores are often squeezed to the utmost to fit the competing demands of spouses and children.

This lack of ultradian synchrony frequently gets translated into squabbles and difficulties among family members. When the typical family comes together at the end of a long day, they have likely spent the entire day ignoring their own ultradian needs and have descended deep into ultradian stress. It is not surprising that conflict arises. Family members are stressed from the events of the day when they have to operate on the outer world's schedule rather than their own. It is no wonder they return home with a great deal of unfinished physical and emotional business, carrying the baggage of the day's unmet personal needs for support and nurturing.

For families, there are three key elements for happier, more positive relationships:

- entraining your circadian and ultradian rhythms together
- being aware of one another's mind–body cues of ultradian stress
- recognizing whenever you have reached a breaking point

Entraining Parent–Child Synchrony

There are many ways for parents with toddlers and school-age children to use ultradian principles throughout the day to bring their family into closer synchrony and avoid the dysfunctional pattens many families unknowingly adopt.

Shared high-activity times. Waking up together is a natural way for the family's rhythms to start the day in synchrony. Even if this is not possible, however, plan to have at least one or two high-activity periods of at least twenty minutes when you play together or are engaged in separate high-energy projects.

Shared eating time. Eating together is one of the basic ways children and parents can reset themselves into ultradian synchrony. Rather than feeding your children first, then eating with your spouse, consider making every meal a shared activity to reharmonize your rhythms.

Shared rest times. If you have several children of various ages, involving any one child in a restful ultradian activity, such as reading or listening to music, can help all the children rebalance their energies and focus. This synchrony can often prevent the usual squabbles and arguments among siblings.

Rocking chairs. One or more children can fit comfortably into a rocker with a parent. The rocking motion helps entrain the parent and children into a relaxing Ultradian Healing Response together.

Story telling. Cuddling up together with a book or nursery story entrains the Ultradian Healing Response in both child and parent. The rhythm of words, pictures, and deep themes can often help family members release pent-up emotions and resolve conflicts.

Other ultradian parent-child entrainers. Among the other activities you can use to enhance parent–child synchrony and provide necessary ultradian rejuvenation are shared hobbies, singing lullabies, and taking a warm bath together.

Even if one or both parents are away from the home most of the day, it is wise to have at least one activity-rest cycle together each day.

Becoming Aware of the Ultradian Stress Syndrome

When families or individual members ignore their need for ultradian rest, they can become subject to a collective version of the Ultradian Stress Syndrome that is an unsuspected source of many family problems. Often this group stress will manifest itself in conflicts whose unconscious intent is to separate family members from each other so they can get time and space alone for the restoration and ultradian healing they need. Signs of such distancing behaviors include:

- being more irritable, emotional, impatient, or hostile
- picking an argument just to break things up so one can be alone during the rest phase of his or her ultradian
- trying to distance oneself behind a newspaper or television set or going off to a room or hobby

Any of these distancing signals indicates that this is not the time to confront family members with problems. Remember, during the Ultradian Stress Syndrome people lose their usual cognitive and verbal skills, patience, and ability to provide emotional support to others. What may seem like a lack of respect or love may actually be an ultradian deficit in social functioning.

When you notice these cues of the Ultradian Stress Syndrome in yourself, explain yourself directly to others: "I need to take a break now. I'm going to lie down for twenty minutes, so please don't interrupt." That way, you won't be tempted to take your stressful feelings out on those around you, and they will better support your need for an Ultradian Healing Response.

Families can also become more vulnerable and dependent on one another when in need of a healing 20-minute ultradian break: family members may exhibit behavior that signals an unconscious dependency and yearning for rest, succor, or support. This dependent behavior may be manifest as:

- wanting to talk or cuddle
- seeking others for help and emotional support on seemingly small matters
- becoming more emotionally sensitive to each other's moods
- becoming more dependent on others' approval and reactions

Many children often become more dependent and cranky when they are overtired and the rest phase of their ultradian rhythm begins. When you notice such cues of the Ultradian Stress Syndrome, you know that these children are going through a natural ultradian shift. They are not being clinging or difficult on purpose. They are usually not even aware of what their regressive behavior means. Their behavior is often not a reflection of an emotional problem, but a result of their natural ultradian need for a brief period of rest and recovery.

At these times, you may want to suggest a quiet activity to facilitate the Ultradian Healing Response that children need— listening to a story, taking a nap, or doing something else undemanding and relaxing. If they do not accept your suggestions for such obvious rest, simply allow them to escape to find their own style of ultradian restoration for the time being.

When your partner, child, or parent is in the ultradian rest and healing phase, this is that person's important time to do inner rejuvenation, so be mindful not to intrude on it. Intruding only turns a period of potential healing into the Ultradian Stress Syndrome.

Recognizing the Breaking Point

When we subject ourselves to the Ultradian Stress Syndrome, it becomes all too easy to take our fatigue and irritation out on those nearest to us. We seem to be prone to the greatest frequency of domestic quarrels, difficulties, and even abuse after 3:00 or 4:00 in the afternoon, when we experience the breaking point as the troughs of our ultradian and circadian rhythms coincide, sending us crashing to the bottom in terms of energy, alertness, and interpersonal skills. Unless you have attended to your ultradian needs regularly throughout the day, there is a strong tendency to fall into malfunction junction and the rebellious body. For family harmony, it is especially crucial that everyone be encouraged to take twenty minutes off at this time.

On weekends and other occasions when the family is together during the day, it helps to support family harmony with a series of nurturing activities after 3:00 or 4:00 in the afternoon. Anything that feels pleasant and relaxing is probably good. Quiet, self-nurturing activities for the family might include:

- quiet games and story times
- sharing the day's experiences with family members
- a favorite hobby that is not demanding
- helping kids with homework
- light socializing
- reading, sewing, or knitting
- gardening or flower arranging
- listening to or playing music
- meditation and walking
- watching television, as long as the program is relaxing and supportive
- playing with pets

ULTRADIANS AND TEENS

Adolescents present profound issues of ultradian stress and change in the family. These years of self-consciousness, a search for self-identity, a changing mind–body, and chaotic emotions require a calm port. The Ultradian Healing Response can facilitate vital self-knowledge and inner peace for the developing adolescent.

Among the enormous mind–body changes of adolescence are changes in circadian and ultradian rhythms. Adolescents occasionally need to be awake at night and asleep in the daytime or seek their own quiet time in the afternoon. They are not being contrary purposely; some shifts in sleep, activity–rest, and eating rhythms can be their natural way of adapting to the hormonal shifts of puberty. As much as possible, the aware parent will encourage teens in setting their own pace and schedule, within reasonable limits. While an occasional all-night party may be an important step in building identity with peers, regular sleep patterns at night and a few ultradian rejuvenations throughout the day can be equally vital for teens if they wish to keep up with the tremendous changes taking place within.

Encourage teens to be aware of their own mind–body rhythms and to schedule accordingly. If they have homework or chores, they may need guidance in finding the peaks and troughs of their ultradian cycles. For your part, consider that the lawn doesn't have to be mowed when your child is engaged in an ultradian recuperative period—it can be done later, when he or she has regained energy.

Equally important, try to give your own attention when a teen needs it. If your teenager comes to you with questions or concerns, it suggests that he or she is in the emotionally available phase of an ultradian rhythm. Now is a prime time to facilitate a constructive behavior change, ethical training, or serious discussion of emotion-laden issues. When parents are unaware of these ultradian peak moments, they typically respond, "Not now, I'm busy," and so foreclose the precious opportunity for communication and learning.

As the adult, you may be more adaptable with your personal ultradian needs than is your teenager. Even if you are moving into your Ultradian Healing Response at the moment your teenager happens to need attention, you may be in a better position to shift your rhythm briefly in order to facilitate communication between you. Teenagers are not yet as skilled as you are in using their own natural moments of openness and self-healing, so take advantage of what may be for them a prime moment of receptivity and change.

ULTRADIANS AND SENIORS

Although 20-minute healing breaks are important for every member of the family, they are absolutely vital for seniors. Proper ultradian rejuvenation can make the difference between becoming frail and senile and being happy and fulfilled in the golden years of life.

Unfortunately, many people in our culture carry negative stereotypes about seniors' needs for rest and rejuvenation. Our society interprets the natural changes of aging as a sign of waning powers. We believe that vitality is everything and that slowness is shameful. Needing to recuperate is seen as a failure and certainly nothing to be encouraged or indulged.

Such attitudes contribute to the negative pressures experienced by many seniors. In their efforts to stay lively and highly functional, some seniors may actually push themselves further into the Ultradian Stress Syndrome. They may need more frequent Ultradian Healing Responses to restore themselves but feel guilty about that need. They are thus more likely to fall into a low amplitude dysrhythmia wherein they are neither fully awake nor fully resting or asleep. They are stuck in a restless limbo of the Ultradian Stress Syndrome where they want to do things but cannot get up quite enough energy, and those around them mistake this for another of the signs of old age.

It is no coincidence that virtually all the classic complaints of elderly people resemble the natural repercussions all of us experience when we fall into the Ultradian Stress Syndrome: short attention span, absent-mindedness, day dreaming, irritability, forgetfulness, fatigue, and disorientation. The older we get, the more vital our ultradian restoration becomes. For seniors, ultradian rejuvenation lives up to its name: it helps them feel and function younger.

The first step to ultradian awareness for seniors—and for those who live with them—is a renewed sensitivity to their mind–body cues. In fact, research from the French National Institute of Health and Medical Research shows that the frequency and strength of ultradian rhythms significantly changes with age. Mind–body rhythms that once moved together fall out of their natural patterns of coordination. Just as with teens, senior citizens may experience natural shifts in their ultradian and circadian rhythms. Seniors therefore need to relearn how to optimize the peaks and troughs of their natural ultradian rhythms. Following are some suggestions for doing so.

Stay Active in Your Peaks

During the ultradian high, it appears to be vital to do something engaging and motivating for your brain and body: walking, exercising, working on interesting tasks, or engaging in stimulating social interaction. Such activity helps to avoid chronically passive states that can lead to further fatigue and depression. You need to experience your performance highs for continuing health now, just as you did for survival in the world of work in your earlier life.

Always allow for creative flexibility in the timing of your day's periods of activity and rest. If something exciting comes up, don't worry about skipping an occasional ultradian rejuvenation period. The extra charge of an exciting social event can help potentiate an ultradian peak period.

Pay Attention to Your Ultradian Healing Response

At the same time, it is equally important to make use of the Ultradian Healing Response for meaningful rest and healing. Several research studies have documented the many uses served by naps and ultradian breaks as recommended in this book.

Morning naps and their meanings. Research suggests that morning naps tend to contain more rapid-eye-movement (REM) sleep than slow-wave sleep. Morning naps are therefore a good time for dream sleep, which decreases during the aging process. This makes morning naps the optimum time for tuning in to the deep patterns of meaning-making and life review that take place during dreams. This meaning synthesis is just as important for healthy senior psychology as identity creation is for the teen.

The often noticed tendency for seniors to reminisce, to go over events of their earlier life, is not a sign of senility, as popular misconceptions have it. The psychologist C. G. Jung believed that most people are so pressured for performance in the real world that they do not have time to find meaning in the first half of their lives. The second half of life, particularly as one approaches death, therefore becomes a period when one needs to find an overall meaning. Jung called this quest for meaning individuation. Reviewing your memories in your senior years is a signal of a new stage of the individuation process whereby you synthesize patterns of meaning in your life as a whole.

Afternoon naps and youthfulness. Recently researchers conducted a study of the rejuvenating effects of injected growth hormone on seniors in their seventies. Subjects in these studies report looking, feeling, and behaving as if they are ten to twenty years younger. Unfortunately, the procedure is still an experimental one, requiring medical supervision and three injections a week, costing about twelve thousand dollars a year. In addition, whether there are any significant side effects is not yet known.

Current research, however, reveals that growth hormone may be released in significant amounts during afternoon naps that last at least an hour. As we age, we tend to have less of the deepest slow-wave sleep (SWS) at night. Afternoon naps can help some people catch up on their much-needed SWS and the pulse of growth hormone that accompanies it. Your afternoon nap may thus be the safest and most reliable fountain of youth we have at the present time.

Ultradian breaks and memory. In addition, ultradian recuperation has been found to help memory in seniors. In a Stanford University study, psychiatric researchers found that a short relaxation period significantly improved the performance of seniors ages sixty-two to eighty-three on tasks involving memory. It also reduced the participants' anxiety about memory, contributing to better performance. In the fourth stage of the Ultradian Healing Response, seniors often reported that they could recall things that had escaped them before taking their 20-minute ultradian rejuvenation break.

One dramatic demonstration of the benefits of ultradian rejuvenation for seniors came at a recent national psychological symposium. Edna, a white-haired woman in her eighties, told me she had attended several lectures about ultradian healing:

Hearing these ideas gave me the courage to take time for the restoration I need. I used to feel so badly. I knew I was tired and needed a rest, but I fought it, because I knew everyone else in the house was worried about me, watching, afraid I was getting senile. So I tried to stay active and alert all the time. But the result was that I was never really fully awake. I felt dopey all the time. My children acted like they thought I was getting Alzheimer's or something—and I wondered if they were right.

Now when that feeling of dopiness comes on, I just let myself go into it. I go to my room, lie down, and do an Ultradian Healing Response. I feel like a new person. I really enjoy my waking periods, I don't just sit there and pretend I am okay. Now I am really awake when I'm awake. I can be available to my family in ways I haven't been for years. I can actually play and enjoy my grandchildren.

Edna's story holds true for all seniors: you simply cannot afford to skip the benefit to be gained from your Ultradian Healing Response.

Ultradian breaks and sleep problems. The Ultradian Healing Response can also be helpful in remedying problems with sleeplessness that often affect seniors. These spring from the natural changes in body rhythms that accompany age. Brian Lippincott, a therapist in Hollister, California, reports a case in which his use of ultradian healing helped one older woman turn her life around:

Millie was a 68-year-old woman afflicted by persistent insomnia. For nine months she had slept less than 4 ½ hours per night, and was significantly fatigued, depressed, and irritable. Millie's husband of thirty-eight years told her to "relax," that her problem was "all in your mind," even accused her of actually getting more sleep than she claimed. Millie's doctor prescribed several drugs: the benzodiazapine, Dalmane; the antidepressant, Desyrel; even the barbiturate, Seconal, but Millie did not like their side effects.

As both she and her husband were retired, and her children had moved out, Millie felt she "had nothing important to do," and had often been lying in bed until late morning. She also had stopped eating, meeting friends, and working at regularly scheduled times, and complained of being plagued by anxieties. By the time she came to see me, her moodiness from lack of sleep caused the relationship to deteriorate so much that she and her husband slept in separate rooms, and divorce seemed a very real possibility.

I told her about ultradian rhythm and that every 90 minutes she had a basic rest/activity cycle. Then I taught her to enter the 20-minute natural Ultradian Healing Response trance: "As your eyes close that's a signal that your inner mind will help solve your sleep problem. Orient your inner mind to a time when you slept very well; let your unconscious show you what puts you right to sleep. . . ." After 13 minutes Millie opened her eyes and stretched and talked about seeing colors and being very relaxed.

For one week she tried a new schedule, taking one ultradian break between 11:00–11:30 A.M. and between 2:30–3:00 P.M. She returned reporting much less irritability and better daytime energy, but was only sleeping a little better.

In the second week, she said "My daytime energy is so good that I have my husband doing ultradian healing too. It structures our day and I have been eating regular meals and bike riding." Her mood and energy were back to normal, yet she still had trouble falling asleep.

By week three, she took three ultradian breaks each day: one at 9:00–9:30 A.M., one after lunch between 12:30–1:30 P.M., and one between 4:30 and 5:30 P.M. before making dinner.

Millie returned elated. She had gone to sleep within 15–30 minutes and had slept straight through to 6:30 A.M. each night. She said, "With these breaks, I'm not tired; it's like six hours sleep is all I need." She reported the first break lasted about 15 minutes and the others 20–30 minutes. She would just lie down and relax and then get up "when I felt like it." Her life has also become more regular and she is now able to baby-sit her grandchildren two evenings per week.

At the successful conclusion of the case, Lippincott wrote in his clinical case notes: "By following the natural Ultradian Healing Response rhythms, Millie was able to re-establish her basic rest–activity cycle, letting her fall asleep easily. Psychologically, the energy provided by these breaks caused higher self-esteem, allowing her to restructure her life. Her ultradian healing periods demonstrated to her and her husband that it was not all in her mind and she was just not 'pulling his leg.' She was able to gain control by following the natural rhythm of life."

For seniors, as for others, there are special benefits in enhanced energy levels, resilience, mental and physical functioning, and self-growth when they take advantage of the healing, restorative potential that comes from heeding their ultradian rhythms.

9

THE SYNCHRONY
OF LOVE:

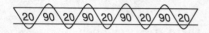

The Ultradian–Sex Connection

Since ancient times, the rites of spring have reflected our seasonal awakening of heightened sexual activity. We now know there are monthly, daily, and hourly rhythms of sexual interest that press for expression in one way or another. In the deepest sense, when we are in synchrony with our sexuality, we are in resonance with some of the most profound imprints of the cosmos within us.

It is ironic that sex—that most pleasurable of human interactions—can so often be marred by conflict and tension. How often have couples experienced the desynchrony that comes when one partner is more or less ready than the other because each has differing levels of arousal and relaxation? Left unresolved, sexual issues can create serious conflict between partners, setting the stage for dissatisfaction and infidelity.

By understanding the rhythmic basis of sexuality, not only can we enhance our relationships, but we can find new ways of tuning in to our mind–body with heightened sensitivity to facilitate health and well-being. In this chapter we begin by exploring our new understanding of the rhythmic basis of sexuality. We can then put into practice a fascinating array of novel approaches to enhance our intimate relationships and sexual lives on many levels.

LIFE RHYTHMS OF SEXUALITY: THE SEASONS

We can witness the changing seasons of sexuality in the life rhythms of nature all around us. We see many of these influences most dramatically in those animals that have obvious seasonal breeding cycles. The lengthening days activate waves of mind–body messenger molecules that awaken sexual patterns of behavior.

That human sexuality is also modulated by these infradian seasonal shifts is now well documented. Spring fever is a real phenomenon that most of us experience to some extent. (Not for nothing do college students gather en masse during spring break.)

Recent research confirms that there is a heightened level of activity and sexuality in spring and summer. The increasing length of daylight influences the pineal gland (the third eye of ancient fame) in the brain, which releases the hormonal messenger melatonin during the night hours. This seasonal change in melatonin leads to an increase in the size of the male's testes in the spring; this, in turn, leads to heightened levels of testosterone, increased sexual activity, and the highest rates of human births in the late winter. (There is also a second peak in the fall, leading to the second-highest rate of birth during the spring.) This suggests an evolutionary origin designed to increase infant survival rates, since children born in the late winter months would be going through the most critical period of early infancy during the spring and summer, when food is most available.

The infradian–sex link is particularly noticeable by many women undergoing the hormonal shifts in many mind–body messenger molecules associated with their monthly cycles.

This case, quoted from a patient's diary and contributed by Donna Spencer, a psychologist in St. Louis, exemplifies the awareness some women can have of their infradian rhythms.

> One night last month, I was very intent on finishing the final chapter of a book I had been reading since 8:00 A.M., yet my eyes began to droop and my concentration to wane. I forced myself to keep reading, yet I realized that an ultradian was coming on, so I thought I'd best just close my eyes for a moment. Just as I sighed and closed my eyes, I was aware of the feeling of a mucus-like substance in my fallopian tube with the accompanying familiar feelings of sensitivity and receptivity. I thought, "Oh, I must be ovulating." As I relaxed more, I was even more aware of an immense feeling of warmth and lubrication in my genital area. If I were twenty-six, this would be the exact time to become impregnated.

I can think of no more vivid example of how a heightened sensitivity to a woman's natural changing states during monthly hormonal shifts reflects our awareness of mind–body rhythms. Here again also, we witness how the Ultradian Healing Response can be a window of access to the messages of the mind–body.

As mentioned earlier, however, whenever an aspect of life is rhythmic, it tends to be adaptable to changing circumstances. As a result, humans have wider variations in the periodicity of their hormonal messenger molecules and sexual behavior than do animals. In our culture we respond more to psychosocial cues and customs than to the amount of light and warmth in the physical environment.

CIRCADIAN AND ULTRADIAN RHYTHMS OF SEXUALITY

While the seasonal rhythms of sexuality have been obvious for centuries, it is only recently that we have recognized the effect of circadian and ultradian rhythms on sexuality. Research suggests that in women the time from 10:00 P.M. to midnight is when conception may be most likely. Men show their own sexual schedules, with a marked daily peak in the male sex hormone testosterone between 8:00 and 9:00 each morning, when blood levels of testosterone run about 40 percent higher than at midnight. Throughout the day, the hormonal and central nervous-system changes brought by our ultradian rhythms also create as many as half a dozen periods of heightened sexual interest, arousal, fantasy, and energy.

Our 90-minute sexual rhythm, like many others, was originally discovered in association with the rapid-eye-movement (REM) dream periods of sleep. During dreaming in REM sleep, men have penile erections and women manifest an analogous tumescence and lubrication of their sexual organs. These are the outward signs of the ultradian coordination of hormones, brain activity, and sexual behavior.

In waking, this same rhythm is manifested in fantasies, particularly sexual fantasies, every ninety minutes or so. Sigmund Freud recognized that sexual fantasies tend to occur during the hypnoidal states when we experience absence of mind—the times we now know reflect the mind–body changes brought by our ultradian rhythm. This sexual arousal can be seen quite clearly in adolescents, who are particularly aware of periodic waves of sexual feelings throughout the day, as their ultradian rhythms bring changes in their hormone levels (estrogen for females; testosterone for males) and mind–body activation.

Adults are most likely to be aware of their sexual feelings and thoughts as they enter the Ultradian Healing Response. This is the time when we are most apt to switch brain hemispheres, turning to our more holistic, fantasy-oriented right brain. Indeed, this may be the time when that mutual fascination and entrainment we call falling in love takes place, since during the trough of our ultradian rhythms we feel open and more easily swept off our feet.

The Ultradian Sex–Stress Link

We also now know that there is an important ultradian link between stress and sexuality, the implications of which we are only beginning to explore. While most sex manuals emphasize that stress and anxiety of any sort reduce sexual interest and performance, the ultradian dynamics of the process were largely not understood.

Robert Sampolsky of Stanford University studied the ways stress, social status, and attitude are related to testosterone levels in baboons. He found the average levels of testosterone are essentially the same when dominant and subordinate male baboons are at rest. However, when they are exposed to stress, their testosterone levels change dramatically. In this case, the stress was the situation of being captured in the wild and subjected to anesthesia so these tests could be performed. Testosterone increased significantly for the dominant animals but decreased for the subdominant animals. The major effect of this sex–stress link typically took place within a 90-to-120-minute period.

What is most fascinating about this study is that the animals' social dominance (such as their likelihood of initiating a fight with a rival, or the likelihood of displacing aggression after losing a fight) as well as their sexual behavior are intimately associated with their emotional style of coping with stress. This appears to confirm the most recent ideas in human psychology that how we react to stress is more important than the number of social stresses to which we are subjected.

ULTRADIAN PATHS TO BETTER SEXUALITY

Given these clear rhythmic links underlying our sexual arousal and behavior, it follows that getting in touch with our ultradian rhythms can enhance both our sexuality and general well-being. Because we live in a largely sex-negative culture, in which most of us have grown up with messages—from family, church, school, and society—that we should be ashamed of our mind–body's natural sexual urges and drives, we are raised to inhibit most of our natural sexual arousal and desire, for fear that it will overwhelm us. Our societal programming is so strong that we often lose touch with these messages completely.

This sexual suppression is a major source of stress for many people, creating a vicious circle of guilt-ridden sexuality and increasing stress. But by becoming more attuned to and aware of our libido, we can learn how to accept and channel it appropriately, making it less likely that we will be controlled by it or compulsively act it out. Ultradian awareness reawakens our connection to the natural sexual messages that rise to our conscious awareness and allows us to reestablish contact with our sexuality. Opening doors to the mind–body during the Ultradian Healing Response can help us access our sexual interest and responsiveness.

We will explore two areas in which our ultradian awareness can improve our sexual lives: to increase intimacy between partners and to heighten the sexual union.

USING ULTRADIANS TO ENHANCE INTIMACY

The first implication of our ultradian knowledge is for couples to use the Ultradian Healing Response to increase emotional intimacy. Research has documented that marital partners working on substantially different schedules are likely to have more than their share of arguments. Their conflicting schedules virtually ensure that they will spend a large portion of their time together in ultradian desynchrony. One partner will be in a trough, needing comfort and rejuvenation, just when the other is at a peak and raring to go.

However, clinical observation suggests that couples with intimate relationships tend to spontaneously integrate their ultradian rhythms and have evolved their own individual entraining tools. Their general activity levels, appetite, need for diversion, and sexual rhythms all occur in synchrony.

Unhappy couples invariably report conflict and desynchrony across these areas.

Following are some suggestions for ways spouses or mates can use their knowledge of ultradian rhythms to increase intimacy.

Morning Synchronization

A pleasant way to start each day is with the custom of sharing morning ultradians. Upon awakening, you each return from a wonderful inner voyage of nighttime dreams and unconscious activity. Sharing with each other what has happened in your dreams and mental life since you went to bed thereby becomes a form of entraining, by which you synchronize mind–body support for each other. Begin by asking your mate open-ended questions, such as:

What were your dreams?

What were your first feelings and thoughts on awakening?

What are you looking forward to in your day?

What is the best you hope to accomplish today?

Reestablishing this contact after the inner focus of the night's journey is a pleasant and effective way to confirm your togetherness for the day. More importantly, clarifying what you hope the day will bring can actually set in motion a positive self-fulfilling prophesy.

Evening Synchronization

Years ago, at the end of a day in almost any town or farm in this country, one could see couples sitting together in rocking chairs on the porch, gazing out across the open fields. Unwittingly they were entraining each other and synchronizing their circadian and ultradian rhythms. The shared quiet and rocking rhythm were also lowering their levels of stress and reducing the odds that they would be projected outward on their mates.

Today, at the end of a day, many couples rush home, quickly prepare dinner, eat, and then turn to television for a few hours of respite and relaxation from a stressful day. What they are missing, however, is a vital moment to tune in to each other's natural rhythms and feelings. Here are some ways to regain your synchrony in the evening:

- greeting each other with a hug and kiss, thereby using touch to entrain yourselves
- enjoying a meal and music together
- lying down doing an Ultradian Healing Response together
- sharing a warm bath and massage
- going for a quiet stroll together
- puttering around the garden or house together

In each of these acts, both nonverbal and verbal cues serve to synchronize your ultradian rhythms and renew your intimate bonds after a day apart. These may seem like simple social acts—and they are—but they also naturally facilitate the Ultradian Healing Response.

Ultradian Discovery Weekends

Weekends can function like vacations for many busy couples. These relatively unscheduled days are a chance to get back into sync with our natural ultradian and circadian rhythms. You may never have suspected that lying lazily in the hammock or at the beach or taking quiet family time was ultradian rejuvenation. In such moments, you are doing exactly what you need to do to replenish and rebalance your mind–body systems.

Because weekends are such prime ultradian time, their entraining effect can be heightened every so often by an ultradian discovery weekend in which couples take time to synchronize together using many ultradian tools—joint meals, activities, massage, baths, sexual play, and relaxation. Either at home or away, spending such time separate from the stresses of everyday life can reharmonize their rhythms.

There is one caveat about your ultradian discovery weekend, however. Our natural circadian (daily) rhythm of sleeping and waking is actually twenty-five hours. It is not a 24 hour cycle coinciding exactly with the planet's day, and many researchers believe the extra hour is a period of flexibility built into us by nature. This means that it is harmless to stay up late on a weekend night to a certain extent, but by extending this time beyond a few hours you can begin to introduce desynchrony in your circadian rhythm. How late can we stay up and still be safe? Only about two hours. If you normally go to sleep at 11:00 P.M., it is best not to push your night out past 1:00 A.M. Some people, of course, have more flexibility in their circadian rhythm and will experience no discomfort in altering it, but those who are more sensitive may find themselves feeling the Monday morning blues a bit more acutely if they shift their circadian clock more than two hours.

ULTRADIAN ENHANCED SEXUALITY

One of the greatest problems that plague sexual partners occurs when one is ready and interested and the other isn't. If this desynchrony occurs often, the sexual union may sour. The result can be unhappy sex, hurtful sex, nonreciprocal sex—and perhaps the eventual avoidance of sex altogether.

Sexual desynchrony can occur for several reasons.

Mismatched phases of the circadian cycle. Sometimes one person doesn't really enjoy sex at the same time of day the other does. The ensuing tension is an example of how out-of-sync sexuality can diminish the pleasure of sex for one or both partners.

Mismatched phases of the ultradian rhythm. In this desynchrony, one partner is in the mood for comforting, nurturing contact while the other is in the mood for exciting, aggressive sex.

Ultradian stress. In this case, one partner is feeling too tired, fragile, or psychologically vulnerable to fully participate in or enjoy the sexual act.

In each of these cases, your ultradian awareness will act as a pathway to sexual synchrony and enhance your sex life by:

- helping you to recognize the emotional cues that indicate you and your partner are in a similarly receptive phase of the natural Ultradian Healing Response
- providing tools to help you synchronize, or entrain, your rhythms so you both move into a state of maximal sexual openness and comfort
- opening doors to your own sexual awareness through accessing the mind–body during the Ultradian Healing Response
- relieving stress or anxiety concerning sex through accessing and creatively reframing past sexual traumas

Ultradian sensitivity helps you consciously enter the natural synergy that happens when partners share the same readiness for sexual contact. That is when we make the most satisfying sexual and emotional connections. The more we can enhance our shared receptivity, the greater our chances for mutually satisfying, passionate intimacy—the best of what sex can and should be.

There are many ways partners can facilitate the synchronization process. In addition to the recommendations on enhancing intimacy, the following sections offer suggestions to heighten sexual union.

Go on an Ultradian Date

Sexual synchrony is so vital that our culture has evolved a series of complex rituals designed to help partners get in touch. When we observe them in animals, we term them mating rituals. Humans have a much friendlier word for them: dates.

Spending an exciting evening together is an intricate process in which two people's ultradian rhythms become synchronized. From first phone call to late-night goodbyes, we engage in a procession of social cues designed to entrain both people's rhythms into sync, build harmony and rapport, and permit satisfying emotional and sexual intimacy.

Suppose that you and someone special have a date set for Friday night. The demands of your separate workdays may have left you completely out of sync, both with your own inner ultradian rhythm and with your date's. Your evening together will help you get in synchrony with each other. It begins long before you see each other, as each of you goes home to freshen up. The warmth of the shower and familiar quiet surroundings help you find the inner comfort and restoration of a vitally important Ultradian Healing Response to recover from the day's stress.

Next, you meet for a drink. Alcohol is an artificial means of inducing the changes in levels of messenger molecules that mimic ultradian healing. Although we definitely do not recommend the use of alcohol, it is a fact of life for many people. The music, and sitting and chatting together all help you entwine ultradian rhythms to maximize interpersonal harmony.

Then comes dinner, a very effective way to naturally facilitate your growing ultradian harmony. Because the hunger rhythm—appetite, oral urges, and stomach pangs—ripples through us each every 90 to 120 minutes, mutually satisfying our need to eat is a potent way to link our rhythms with another person's. It is no accident that socially oriented meals last about an hour and a half, the length of one full ultradian rhythm.

After dinner comes more entertainment activity—a movie, play, or concert. That, too, usually will last between 90 and 120 minutes, one ultradian rhythm. Hollywood has learned by trial and error to respect our 90-to-120-minute ultradian rhythm. If movies are too long, the audience will get restive and bored. That acute master of mood, Alfred Hitchcock, once wrote: "The length of a film should be directly related to the endurance of the human bladder." The great director probably never even knew that his rule had its basis in ultradian biology: urination follows a 90-minute rhythm.

If the entertainment lasts longer than two hours, it will usually have an intermission, an approximately 20-minute break before we resume. An intermission, or *entr'acte,* is the length of one typical ultradian recovery period. In baseball or football, we see the same ultradian need reflected in the seventh-inning stretch or halftime break, when fans get up and move around.

By the end of the typical date, you have come to the end of a complex and lengthy courtship ritual made up of one entrainment process after another. Your rhythms are in sync, your rapport has grown, and you are now as attuned as you will ever be. You feel growing comfort and intimacy as your mind–body rhythms become more closely synchronized. That's what feeling good together means: being in synchrony with each other. Could there be a more natural path to further sexual intimacy?

Sex, Comfort, and the Brain-Breath Link

If an evening out is not to your liking, relaxing together, preferably in a calm, nondistracting environment, will help you tune in more deeply to your natural ultradian rhythms.

When both partners have had busy days, it is helpful for them to spend the evening nurturing themselves, spending three or four hours leisurely getting in sync by engaging in shared activities—such as listening to music—that help to entrain their rhythms.

Before the biological roots of ultradian rhythms were known, sex researchers in the early part of this century stumbled on the use of the Ultradian Healing Response to increase intimacy. Dr. Rudolf von Urban, a pioneer in American sex research, showed that "when lovers relax deeply together, a resonance effect begins to take place between their energy fields that brings profound healing to both." Partners bonded in such deep comfort "can enjoy a long-lasting, whole-body orgasm." This bonding and comfort period, which lasts ten to twenty minutes, is obviously synonymous with the Ultradian Healing Response.

One way to enhance sexual bonding is to use the brain-breath link by lying down together on your right sides in the typical spoon position. The warmth and comfort of this embrace will tend to synchronize your right brain hemispheres together to facilitate intimacy. The synchrony of this brain–breath pattern will promote autonomic-system and hormonal-messenger-molecule balance, which will enhance your emotional togetherness on many levels.

This body posture may also help the initial social process of entraining. You may have noticed a couple courting. As one speaks the other listens, head cocked to one side. We recognize this tipped head as a friendly, attentive pose, suggesting further interest and intimacy. It signals a budding rapport, a cue to increase intimacy.

This tipped-head signal may be a way of inducing the nasal shift and changing the activation of our dominant brain hemisphere. That, in turn, subtly allows us to access a different part of ourselves, perhaps the more emotional, sensual, less analytic side of our personalities. What may have begun as the outer sign of a physical brain shift has become codified into a social cue that we now interpret as a mildly flirtatious, intimate invitation.

Focusing and Fantasizing Together

Another way to use the ultradian approach to enhance intimacy is for couples to spend a few moments quietly together before going into an Ultradian Healing Response period. During this time, look at your partner, and ask yourself, "What are the ways we can increase our intimacy?" Pay attention to what issues come up as you look at and think about your partner.

By focusing like this before entering ultradian healing, you prime your unconscious to offer up insights into the emotional issues that can draw you closer. Then do your Ultradian Healing Response together. Afterward, talk with your partner about your thoughts or feelings so you can decide together how to enhance your sexual life.

Alternatively, you can use your Ultradian Healing Response together to tune in to your partner's personal erotic signals as well as your own. In the unguarded moments of the Ultradian Healing Response, you may become aware of a specific fantasy unfolding in your mind. After you have come out of your relaxing ultradian interlude, share this with your partner so you will be better prepared to enjoy sex together.

There is nothing illicit about our inner fantasies. If your fantasies aren't what you want to actually express in your behavior, that need be no cause for anxiety. It is the role of the unconscious to offer many different possibilities and the role of the conscious mind to select which you want to express. But in order to be able to explore our sexual possibilities, it is important that we do not arbitrarily choke off and limit these messages by imposing rules and restrictions on what we believe we should be thinking or feeling. During the Ultradian Healing Response these suppressed feelings and desires will naturally come to the surface again because our defenses are down.

Some people may be frightened by these surfacing feelings and surprised at what sexual images may come up. One result of negative societal programming about sex is that some people feel haunted or plagued by sexual thoughts. They feel conflicted, ashamed, or intensely anxious about their own sexual feelings, worrying, perhaps, that they are unnatural.

Yet acting out any sexual fantasy is always a matter of choice. It is very important to know that we can all act in a manner consistent with our highest personal ethical standards no matter what information emerges during the Ultradian Healing Response. It may even help to remind yourself: "These sexual thoughts/images/feelings may be the results of the inborn rhythm nature gave me. Having periodic sexual fantasies does not indicate that I have a sexual problem; rather, that I am experiencing the natural sexual component of my inborn ultradian rhythms." As such, these thoughts are not to be resisted, suppressed, or feared but received and meditated upon as any other mind–body message. You never have to kill the messenger; you are in control. You can take all the time you need to evaluate the message and decide what to do with it.

Ultradian fantasy is your inner experimental theater, where you can try out new ideas and images of your sexual possibilities. This period of reverie gives you a lovely, safe, private place to explore whatever you want. What happens here is just for you—nobody else need ever know about it. Your conscious mind can later decide whether, when, how, and with whom it is appropriate to express your fantasies. Our awareness of our sexual fantasies and sensations are gifts we are offered by our inner sensual mind. Cultivate them, for they mean you have opened the pathway to your inner being and have touched its endless resources for greater satisfaction and enjoyment as a sexual being.

Touch and Foreplay

Touch may be the most powerful sociobiological signal of all. When we are touched gently and rhythmically, our brains release the feel-good messenger molecules called beta-endorphins and we slip into the psychologically receptive state of the Ultradian Healing Response. We open up to increased intimacy. No wonder that the people we let touch us—massage and physical therapists, barbers and hairdressers, nurses and physicians—are often the recipients of our deepest personal confidences.

In our own culture, sex usually begins with touching or petting. By hugging, kissing, and massage, we are using our vast sensory channels of touch to entrain our ultradian mind—body links to comfort and sexuality, bringing our partner and ourself to the same level of sexual responsiveness.

From the ultradian perspective, foreplay is another way to facilitate ultradian synchrony. From a reproductive standpoint, sexual synchrony increases the odds that we will mate successfully and perpetuate the species. Given the source of ultradian rhythms in the human chromosome, one could say that the instructions for foreplay are written in our very genes.

This new ultradian understanding explains several long-observed facts about foreplay. Sex manuals have maintained that a minimum period of ten to twenty minutes is necessary to put us in synchrony for the best sex. In ultradian terms, this is the time we need to entrain and synchronize both partners' rhythms; not coincidentally, it is the same length of time as the Ultradian Healing Response.

Lovers who take the time to get in sync through foreplay are helping themselves, and their partners, have a more satisfying sexual interaction. Sexual problems such as impotence, premature ejaculation, and dyspareunia (painful intercourse in women) may be at least partially caused by lack of attention to the crucial step of synchronizing the ultradian sexual rhythms of both partners.

If you are about to make love and are not sufficiently aroused (in women, having insufficient lubrication; in men, lacking an erection), this is a mind—body signal that you need to get into deeper ultradian harmony and synchronize rhythms with your lover. Simply accept these physical signs as gentle ultradian reminders to enjoy foreplay for a while longer, allowing your sexual rhythms to build to a natural climax together.

SEX OVER SIXTY

Ultradian approaches can also be a wonderful sexual facilitator for older couples whose ultradian rhythms are undergoing significant alteration and adjustment. Women, for example, may experience less natural sexual lubrication with age. For senior men, while the ability to become erect does not necessarily diminish, it may take longer. And both men and women may take longer to achieve orgasm. Why not enjoy this prolonged period of intimacy as one of the rewards of age? Here are several tips to enhance sex for seniors:

- Allow more preparation time.
- Appreciate the nonorgasmic aspect of sex, focusing on kinesthetic feelings and pleasure in general.
- Take advantage of the warmth of a bubble bath and/or hot tub together.
- Review the best moments of your life together, remembering past experience to turn on sexuality.

For all of us, no matter what our age, the 20-minute Ultradian Healing Response can be a wonderful, new sensual tool for emotional rapport and sexual enhancement. As you enhance your rapport with ultradian synchrony, you will come to agree: couples in ultradian harmony, listening to their own and each other's mind–body signals, can deepen their intimacy and enjoy the most meaningful sexuality of their lives.

10

MANY PATHS, ONE GOAL

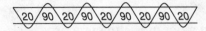

> My fiftieth year had come and gone,
> I sat, a solitary man,
> In a crowded London shop,
> An open book and empty cup
> On the marble table-top.
> While on the shop and street I gazed
> My body of a sudden blazed;
> And twenty minutes more or less
> It seemed, so great my happiness,
> That I was blessed and could bless.
>
> WILLIAM BUTLER YEATS
> *Vacillation*

The Ultradian Healing Response points like a compass to a mysterious something behind many mysteries of human consciousness that have fascinated us for millennia. Across all continents and cultures, humans have historically sought out many paths to states of harmony, healing, and higher awareness. We have developed a myriad of what are termed transpersonal disciplines that attempt to go beyond the boundaries of our everyday human experience. Among them are meditation, yoga, zen, body massage, acupuncture, religious prayer, faith healing, and shamanism; together, they include millions of adherents the world over. To those traditional practices, modern Western researchers have recently added

numerous other techniques: the Relaxation Response pop-
ularized by Dr. Herbert Benson of Harvard University, biofeedback and many so-called methods of mind control,
progressive relaxation, autogenic training, hypnosis, and
imagery, not to mention the 300-plus schools of modern
psychotherapy.

Each of these ancient and modern healing practices has
elaborated its own belief system—medical, spiritual, religious, or philosophical—and developed apparently different,
and even diametrically opposite, means of facilitating healing
or higher consciousness. Each has its own special genius and
value.

Yet, when we delve beneath the creeds, doctrines, and rituals to look at the underlying process of mind–body communication, one common denominator remains: all methods
access and facilitate one aspect or other of our natural 20-
minute Ultradian Healing Response. The Zen monk in meditative silence, the patient stretched on the analyst's couch, the
devout worshiper in fervent prayer, the busy executive taking
a cat nap, the devotee of body massage, the New-Age couple
enjoying a guided visualization—however different their approaches seem to be, they all have far more in common than
they realize. They are following many paths to the same goal:
to access and facilitate our natural ultradian rhythms of
mind–body healing and states of consciousness. The natural
rhythms of consciousness and behavior associated with the
Ultradian Healing Response provide a scientific rationale for
all these approaches.

We can discern ultradian phenomena at work in many reports of shamanistic healing traditions. The shaman's primary
task when attempting to heal people is to distract the sick person's attention from whatever stressful activity or symptom to
which the patient is compulsively tied. The native medicine
man or woman typically engages in attention-focusing activity, putting the subject in a passive role that allows the supposed magic to work. Much of that magic, of course, is in the
simple, natural restoration of the Ultradian Healing Response
that takes place all by itself when we lie down and let go.

Entraining and synchronizing our mind–body rhythms plays a central role in shamanistic healing. The shaman entrains the patient's mind–body rhythms by touch, drumming, dancing, chanting, making smoke, special diets, and drugs. The altered conditions of light and dark, as well as isolation from the typical zeitgebers (time givers) of ordinary everyday life, were used in ancient healing rituals to disrupt the Ultradian Stress Syndrome the patient had unwittingly fallen into. This basic therapeutic ritual disrupts the patient's stress cycle with natural circadian and ultradian rhythms of activity, rest, and healing. This has its modern counterpart in a variety of the healing rituals of most holistic health approaches.

For thousands of years, the entrainment and synchronization of mind–body rhythms has been the common factor in the world's healing therapies. While these methods often succeeded in facilitating healing, the reason why they worked remained obscure. In modern medicine such healing is called the *placebo response*. Only recently have we come to understand that the placebo response actually utilizes many psychosocial cues to entrain the natural mind–body rhythms of what we now call the *Ultradian Healing Response*.

ULTRADIAN PSYCHOTHERAPY

Just as ultradian approaches have been used by many folk healing traditions around the world, they also appear in many modern psychotherapies. Freud, the father of psychoanalysis, knew that when people lie on the analytic couch, they fall into a dreamy, reverie-like state. There, they free-associate about their childhood memories, feelings, dreams, and imagery to access the source of their problems. Now we know that many of these psychoanalytic phenomena—childhood recall, imagery, sexual fantasy, emotional openness, and suggestibility—are the hallmarks of entirely natural mind–body shifts of brain-hemisphere dominance that take place naturally every hour and a half or so for about twenty minutes during our Ultradian Healing Response.

There are four distinct ultradian phases in the typical psychotherapy session:

1. There is an active initial phase during which the client experiences a certain amount of stress as he or she tells the story of the current problem.

2. Then comes that moment of pause when the client looks to the therapist for an answer. This pause and query is a signal that the client is entering the second phase of the therapy session: a natural period of receptivity—the 20-minute Ultradian Healing Response.

3. Within the twenty minutes of the inner access provided by this ultradian window, the client frequently finds some insight and/or experiences some healing.

4. Then the therapist and client together come back to the reality of the here and now to confirm or ratify the therapeutic insights.

Many psychotherapists working within a variety of theoretical orientations will recognize these four stages as typical of a good therapy session.

ULTRADIANS AND HYPNOSIS

Nowhere is the usefulness of the Ultradian Healing Response clearer than in the field of hypnotherapy. Many professional hypnotherapists now believe that there is no such thing as a unique state of therapeutic hypnosis. Instead, they feel that what is commonly called hypnosis may be a matter of entraining people to enter more deeply into natural mind–body states of healing that occur spontaneously during daily life.

There appears to be no phenomenon that we can observe under hypnosis that cannot also be observed as an entirely natural occurrence during the Ultradian Healing Response. In both situations, people may be more suggestible and often report spontaneous experiences of reduced pain (analgesia), altered sensations and perceptions (illusions and hallucinations), shifts in memory (amnesia and hyperamnesia), a sense of comfort and relaxation, time distortion, and many other typical hypnotic phenomena.

When closely examined, the phenomena of the Ultradian Healing Response and clinical hypnosis seem to be two sides of the same therapeutic coin. This new view suggests that we all can master self-hypnosis by learning to facilitate our inborn, Ultradian Healing Response.

ULTRADIANS AND MEDITATION

What one tradition calls meditation, another may call ritual and prayer. No matter what name it is given, we again observe many clear ultradian processes at work. In the teaching of Pir Vilayat Kahn, the spiritual leader of the Sufi Order of the West, for example, it is typical to have beginning meditators sit for a 20-minute visualization or meditation. Similarly, the teachers of Buddhist Zazen meditation instruct students who wish to devote a whole day to meditation to sit for periods of ninety minutes, interspersed with walking meditations lasting about twenty minutes. These practices reflect the ancient teachings of their masters, who observed that novices could easily experience a natural 20-minute meditative state and eventually learn to synchronize their whole day to a meditative 90-to-120-minute activity–rest rhythm.

It may seem a long distance from shamanistic healing to Zen meditation and modern clinical hypnotherapy. Yet from an ultradian perspective, these practices use the same natural doorway to mind–body communication—an ultradian one that opens periodically throughout the day. Over the centuries, each of these traditions has elaborated its own proprietary idiom and metaphor to explain people's experiences of healing and well being. Ultradian theory offers a unifying scientific orientation that can integrate these disparate traditions of healing and consciousness.

To recognize the commonalities of these ancient and modern practices is in no way to diminish the special value of any particular system of belief and healing. Although many traditions and practices ultimately lead to the same or similar goals, each of mankind's myriad paths holds its own unique wonders and revelations, intrinsic to its special insights and practices.

The Ultradian Healing Response offers us a testament to our shared human heritage. All of the Earth's cultures have recognized the same periodic need for ultradian restoration and healing. We can draw inspiration from knowing that in so many of the great spiritual and healing traditions of history, we have been guided with a natural wisdom that science is now beginning to understand.

ULTRADIAN
HEALING
RESPONSE SURVEY

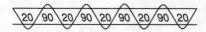

Circle True or False for each of the following questions.

1. My general health has improved with the use of the Ultradian Healing Reponse.   TRUE   FALSE

2. A snack of 200 calories or less taken before rest has improved my Ultradian Healing Response and has calmed my nerves.   TRUE   FALSE

3. The Ultradian Diet has been an important part of my weight-control program.   TRUE   FALSE
Please describe.

_____

_____

_____

_____

4. Emotional harmony and sexual experiences have improved since I began using the Ultradian Healing Response.   TRUE   FALSE

5. I am able to experience *lucid dreaming,* in which I am aware that I am dreaming, and I can sometimes even change my dreams and fantasies during the Ultradian Healing Response.   TRUE   FALSE

6. I have used ultradians breaks to improve my work performance.   TRUE   FALSE
Please describe.

_____

_____

_____

_____

7. I have had significant help with stress reduction since I began using the Ultradian Healing Response a few times a day.   TRUE   FALSE

8. I have had fewer psychosomatic problems since I have been using the Ultradian Healing Response several times a day.   TRUE   FALSE
Please describe.

_____

_____

_____

_____

9. My moods and emotions have improved with the use of the Ultradian Healing Response.   TRUE   FALSE
   Please describe.

   _____

   _____

   _____

10. My memory has improved since I began taking a few ultradian rests every day.   TRUE   FALSE

11. My learning and study skills have improved since I began using the Ultradian Healing Response.   TRUE   FALSE

12. My relationships have improved since I began taking an ultradian break whenever I feel tired or irritable.
    TRUE   FALSE

13. I have been able to improve my personal best in sports with my use of the Ultradian Healing Response to optimize performance.   TRUE   FALSE

14. I experience renewed energy throughout the day when I take an ultradian break whenever I need to.
    TRUE   FALSE

15. The rejuvenation experiences I've had during the Ultradian Healing Response have led me to think, feel, and behave more youthfully.   TRUE   FALSE
    Please describe.

    _____

    _____

    _____

16. I have experienced important insights during the Ultradian Healing Response that have helped me with my life.

TRUE   FALSE

17. I have had rewarding creative experiences during or right after an Ultradian Healing Response.   TRUE   FALSE
Please describe.

_____

_____

_____

_____

_____

18. I have become aware of pain or physical symptoms during an ultradian rest period that I did not know I had.

TRUE   FALSE

Please list any problem or medical condition that has been confirmed by a doctor.

_____

_____

_____

_____

_____

19. I have had unusual experiences and body sensations during the Ultradian Healing Response.   TRUE   FALSE
Please describe.

_____

_____

_____

_____

20. I have used the Ultradian Healing Response to help me end a drug addition.   TRUE   FALSE

Please describe any addictions that you have ended.

_____

_____

_____

_____

21. Ultradians have helped me break bad habits.
    TRUE   FALSE
Please describe.

_____

_____

_____

_____

_____

22. My doctor noticed that some aspect of my health has improved since I began using the Ultradian Healing Response.   TRUE   FALSE
Please describe.

_____

_____

_____

_____

23. I have had some difficulty in trying to use the Ultradian Healing Response.   TRUE   FALSE
Please describe.

_____

_____

_____

24. I am at my best when I use the Ultradian Healing Response _____ number of times each day.

25. I have had spiritual experiences during or right after the Ultradian Healing Response.   TRUE   FALSE
Please describe.

_____

_____

_____

_____

YOUR ULTRADIAN INTENSIVE DIARY

We would be particularly pleased to receive a copy of your Ultradian Intensive Diary as described in chapter four. For one week simply record:

1. the date
2. the times of day when you use the Ultradian Healing Response
3. a few sentences describing each experience

We are interested in learning something about your personal patterns, sensations, feelings, and healing experiences. In short anything that may inspire others and help research plan more detailed studies of the Ultradian Healing Response.

Occupation _____ Education level _____

Age _____ Sex _____

Name, address, and phone number are optional.

Name _____

Address _____

Phone number _____

Please return this completed survey to:

Dr. Ernest Rossi
c/o Jeremy P. Tarcher, Inc.
5858 Wilshire Boulevard, Suite 200
Los Angeles, CA 90036

SOURCES

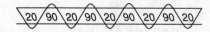

CHAPTER 1 / On the Trail of a Scientific Mystery

A general introduction to the history of depth psychology and hypnosis covering the contributions of Charcot, Janet, Freud, and Jung can be found in:

> Ellenberger, H. (1970) *The Discovery of the Unsconscious.* New York: Basic Books.

An introduction to the works of Milton H. Erickson can be found in:

> Erickson, M. (1980) *The Collected Papers of Milton H. Erickson on Hypnosis (4 vols.),* E. Rossi, (Ed.). New York: Irvington.

The new informational approach to mind-body healing may be found in the following:

> Rossi, E. (1986) *The Psychobiology of Mind-Body Healing: New Concepts of Therapeutic Hypnosis.* New York: W. W. Norton.

> Rossi, E., and Cheek, D. (1988) *Mind-Body Therapy: Ideodynamic Healing in Hypnosis.* New York: W. W. Norton.

> Rossi, E. (1990) From mind to molecule: More than a metaphor, in J. Zeig, and S. Gilligan, (Eds.), *Brief Therapy: Myths, Methods and Metaphors.* New York: Brunner/Mazel.

Sources on the relationship between ultradian rhythms and hypnosis:

> Rossi, E. (1981) Hypnotist describes natural rhythm of trance readiness, *Brain Mind Bulletin* 6(7), 1.

Rossi, E. (1986) Altered states of consciousness in everyday life: The ultradian rhythms, in B. Wolman and M. Ullman (Eds.), *Handbook of Altered States of Consciousness* (pp. 97–132). New York: Van Nostrand.

Rossi, E. (1986) Hypnosis and ultradian rhythms, in B. Zilbergeld, M. Edelstien, and D. Araoz (Eds.), *Hypnosis: Questions and Answers* (pp. 17–21). New York: W. W. Norton.

Rossi, E. (1990) The new yoga of the west: Natural rhythms of mind-body healing. *Psychological Perspectives, 22,* 146–161.

Rossi, E. (1990) The eternal quest. *Psychological Perspectives, 22,* 6–23.

Rossi, E. (1991) The wave nature of consciousness, *Psychological Perspectives, 24,* 1–6.

CHAPTER 2 / The Mind-Body Rhythms of Self-Regulation

A number of volumes on seasonal circadian and ultradian rhythms includes:

Hughes, M. (1989) *Body Clock: The Effects of Time on Human Health.* New York: Facts on File.

Lloyd, D. and Rossi, E. (Eds.) (1992) *High Frequency Biological Rhythms: Functions of the Ultradians.* New York: Springer-Verlag.

Luce, G. (1970) *Biological Rhythms in Psychiatry and Medicine.* U.S. Dept. of Health, Education and Welfare, NIMH.

Rosenthal, N. (1989) *Seasons of the Mind: Why You Get the Winter Blues.* New York: Bantam.

General references in the area of sleep, dreams, and creativity can be found in:

Aserinsky, E. and Kleitman, N. (1953) Regularly occurring periods of eye motility and concomitant phenomena during sleep. *Science, 118,* 273–274.

Kleitman, N. (1963) *Sleep and Wakefulness as Alternating Phases in the Cycle of Existence.* Chicago: University of Chicago Press.

Kleitman, N. (1970) Implications of the rest-activity cycle: Implications for organizing activity, in E. Hartmann (Ed.), *Sleep and Dreaming.* Boston: Little, Brown.

LaBerge, S., and Rheingold, H. (1990) *Exploring the World of Lucid Dreaming.* New York: Ballantine.

Brain, breath, and consciousness references include:

Rossi, E. (1986) Altered states of consciousness in everyday life: The ultradian rhythms, in B. Wolman and M. Ullman (Eds.), *Handbook of Altered States of Consciousness* (pp. 97–132). New York: Van Nostrand.

Werntz, D. (1981) Cerebral hemispheric activity and autonomic nervous function. Doctoral Thesis, University of California, San Diego.

Werntz, D., Bickford, R., Bloom, R., and Shannahoff-Khalsa, D. (1983) Alternating cerebral hemispheric activity and lateralization of autonomic nervous function. *Human Neurobiology, 2,* 39–43.

Memory, learning, and performance are covered in:

Broughton, R. (1975) Biorhythmic variations in consciousness and psychological functions. *Canadian Psychological Review: Psychologie Canadienne, 16* (4), 217–239.

Brown, F., and Graeber, R. (Eds.) (1982) *Rhythmic Aspects of Behavior.* Hillsdale, NJ: Lawrence Erlbaum.

Luce, G. (1970) *Biological Rhythms in Psychiatry and Medicine.* U. S. Dept. of Health, Education and Welfare, NIMH.

Schulz, H., and Lavie, P. (1985) *Ultradian Rhythms in Physiology and Behavior.* New York: Springer-Verlag.

The mind-gene connection is summarized in:

Kandel, E. (1989) Genes, nerve cells, and the remembrance of things past. *Journal of Neuropsychiatry 1*(2), 103–125.

Rossi, E. (1987) From mind to molecule: A state-dependent memory, learning, and behavior theory of mind-body healing. *Advances, 4*(2), 46–60.

Rossi, E. (1990) Mind-molecular communication: Can we really talk to our genes? *Hypnos, 17*(1), 3–14.

Rossi, E. (1990) The new yoga of the west: Natural rhythms of mind-body healing. *Psychological Perspectives, 22,* 146–161.

CHAPTER 3 / Stressing Out

Background research on the relationship between stress and ultradian rhythms includes:

Friedman, S. (1978) A psychophysiological model for the chemotherapy of psychosomatic illness. *The Journal of Nervous & Mental Diseases, 166,* 110–116.

Friedman, S., Kantor, I., Sobel, S., and Miller, R. (1978) On the treatment of neurodermatitis with a monomine oxidase inhibitor. *The Journal of Nervous & Mental Diseases, 166,* 117–125.

Iranmanesh, A., Lizarradle, G., Johnson, M., and Veldhuis, J. (1989) Circadian, ultradian, and episodic release of B-endorphin in men, and its temporal coupling with cortisol. *Journal of Clinical Endocrinology and Metabolism, 68*(6), 1019–1025.

Iranmanesh, A., Veldhuis, J., Johnson, M., and Lizarradle, G. (1989) 24-hour pulsatile and circadian patterns of cortisol secretion in alcoholic men. *J. Androl., 10,* 54–63.

Rossi, E., and Cheek, D. (1988) *Mind-Body Therapy: Ideodynamic Healing in Hypnosis.* New York: W. W. Norton.

Selye, H. (1976) *The Stress of Life.* New York: McGraw-Hill.

Background reading for the ultradian-stress-addiction link includes:

Goldstein, I., Shapiro, D., Hui, K., and Yu, J. (1990) Blood pressure response to the "second cup of coffee." *Psychosomatic Medicine, 52,* 337–345.

Koob, G., and Bloom, F. (1988) Cellular and molecular mechanisms of drug dependence. *Science, 242,*715.

Lane J., Adcock, A., Williams, R., and Kuhn, C. (1990) Caffeine effects on cardiovascular and neuroendocrine responses to acute psychosocial stress and their relationship to level of habitual caffeine consumption. *Psychosomatic Medicine, 52,* 320–336.

Pert, C., Ruff, M., Weber, R., and Herkenham, M. (1985) Neuropeptides and their receptors: A psychosomatic network. *The Journal of Immunology, 135*(2), 820s–826s.

Pert, C., and Ruff, M., Spencer, D., and Rossi, E. (1989) Self-reflective molecular psychology. *Psychological Perspectives, 20*(1), 213–221.

Rossi, E., and Cheek, D. (1988) *Mind-Body Therapy: Ideodynamic Healing in Hypnosis.* New York: W. W. Norton.

Schaef, A. (1987) *When Society Becomes an Addict.* San Francisco: Harper & Row.

Schaef, A., and Fassel, D. (1988) *The Addictive Organization.* San Francisco: Harper & Row.

Torsvall, L., and Akerstedt, T. (1988) Disturbed sleep while being on-call: An EEG study of ships' engineers. *Sleep, 11*(1), 35.

CHAPTER 4 / The 20-minute break

Background research for the Ultradian Healing Response includes:

Broughton, R. (1975) Biorhythmic variations in consciousness and psychological functions. *Canadian Psychological Review: Psychologie Canadienne, 16*(4), 217–239.

Dinges, D., and Broughton, R. (1989) *Sleep and Alertness.* New York: Raven Press.

Klein, R., Pilon, D., Prosser, S. and Shannahoff-Khalsa, D. (1986) Nasal airflow asymmeteries and human performance, *Biological Psychology, 23,* 127–137.

Kleitman, N. (1969) Basic rest-activity cycle in relation to sleep and wakefulness, in A. Kales (Ed.), *Sleep: Physiology & Pathology* (pp. 33–38). Philadelphia: Lippincott.

Kleitman, N. (1970) Implications of the rest-activity cycle: Implications for organizing activity, in E. Hartmann (Ed.), *Sleep and Dreaming*. Boston: Little, Brown.

Kupfer, D., Monk, T., and Barchas, J. (1988) *Biological Rhythms and Mental Disorders*. New York: Guilford.

Libet, B. (1985) Unconscious cerebral initiative and the role of conscious will in voluntary action. *The Behavioral and Brain Sciences, 8, 529–566.*

Rossi, E. (1972/1985) *Dreams and the Growth of Personality.* New York: Brunner/Mazel.

Rossi, E. (1986) Altered states of consciousness in everyday life: The ultradian rhythms, in B. Wolman and M. Ullman (Eds.), *Handbook of Altered States of Consciousness* (pp. 97–132). New York: Van Nostrand.

Rossi, E. (1986) Hypnosis and ultradian rhythms, in B. Zilbergeld, M. Edelstien, and D. Araoz (Eds.), *Hypnosis: Questions and Answers* (pp. 17–21), New York: W. W. Norton.

CHAPTER 5 / The Ultradian Toolbox

Many of the ultradian tools discussed in this chapter evolved out of my earlier work with Milton H. Erickson:

Erickson, M., Rossi, E., and Rossi, S. (1976) *Hypnotic Realities.* New York: Irvington.

Erickson, M., and Rossi, E. (1979) *Hypnotherapy: An Exploratory Casebook.* New York: Irvington.

Erickson, M., and Rossi, E. (1981). *Experiencing Hypnosis: Therapeutic Approaches to Altered States.* New York: Irvington.

Erickson, M., and Rossi, E. (1989) *The February Man: Evolving Consciousness and Identity in Hypnotherapy.* New York: Brunner/Mazel.

Rossi, E., and Ryan M. (Eds.) (1986) *Mind-Body Communication in Hypnosis. Vol. 3. The Seminars, Workshops, and Lectures of Milton H. Erickson.* New York: Irvington.

Rossi, E., and Ryan M. (Eds.) (1990) *Creative Choice in Hypnosis. Vol. 4. The Seminars, Workshops, and Lectures of Milton H. Erickson,* New York: Irvington.

Rossi, E., Ryan, M., and Sharp, F. (Eds.) (1984) *Healing in Hypnosis. Vol. 1. The Seminars, Workshops, and Lectures of Milton H. Erickson.* New York: Irvington.

Rossi, E., and Ryan, M. (1991) *Creative Choice in Hypnosis. Vol. 4 The Seminars, Workshops, and Lectures of Milton H. Erickson.* New York: Irvington.

General aspects of ultradian and circadian rhythms and jet lag can be found in:

Campbell, J. (1986) *Winston Churchill's Afternoon Nap.* New York: Touchstone.

Coleman, R. (1986) *Wide Awake at 3 A.M.: By Choice or Chance.* New York: Freedman.

Literature on the brain–breath connection has been cited previously in the notes on chapter two.

The significance of psychosocial cues in entraining mind–body rhythms has been emphasized in the following:

Rossi, E. (1991) The wave nature of Consciousness. *Psychological Perspectives,* 1–6.

Wever, R. (1979) *The Circadian System of Man.* New York: Springer-Verlag.

CHAPTER 6 / Maximizing Performance

The more technical literature in this area includes:

Akerstedt, T. (1988) Sleepiness as a consequence of shift work. *Sleep, 11*(1), 17–34.

Klein, R., and Armitage, R. (1979) Rhythms in human performance: 1-1/2 hour oscillations in cognitive style. *Science, 204,* 1326–1328.

Mitler, M., et al. (1988) Catastrophes, sleep, and public policy: Consensus report. *Sleep, 11*(1), 100–109.

National Transportation Safety Board. (1986) Annual Review of Aircraft Accident Data. U.S. Government report PB89-151-21.

Schulz, H., and Lavie, P. (1985) *Ultradian Rhythms in Physiology and Behavior.* New York: Springer-Verlag.

Torsvall, L., and Akerstedt, T. (1988) Disturbed sleep while being on-call: An EEG study of ships' engineers. *Sleep, 11*(1), 35–38.

Webb, W. (1982) *Biological Rhythms, Sleep, and Performance.* New York: John Wiley & Sons.

Winget, C., DeRoshia, W., and Holley, D. Circadian rhythms and athletic performance. *Medicine and Science in Sports and Exercise, 17*(5), 498–516.

Background reading on ultradian rhythms and mood, memory, and performance include:

Pert, C., Ruff, M., Weber, R., and Herkenham, M. (1985) Neuropeptides and their receptors: A psychosomatic network. *The Journal of Immunology, 135*(2) 820s–826s.

Rossi, E. (1990) From mind to molecule: More than a metaphor, in J. Zeig, and S. Gilligan, (Eds.), *Brief Therapy: Myths, Methods and Metaphors.* New York: Brunner/Mazel.

Rossi, E., and Ryan, M. (Eds.) (1986) *Mind–Body Communication in Hypnosis. Vol. 3. The Seminars, Workshops, and Lectures of Milton H. Erickson.* New York: Irvington.

Research on ultradian rhythms, performance, and the *breaking point* was reported by:

Kaufmann, E. (1989) The new rhythms of fitness. *American Health,* December 1989.

Toufexis, A. (1990) Drowsy America. *Time.* December 17, 1990.

Tsuji, Y., and Kobayshi, T. (1988) Short and long ultradian EEG components in daytime arousal. *Electroencephalography and Clinical Neurophysiology, 70,* 110–117.

CHAPTER 7 / Ultradians and Diet, Weight Control, and Addictions

Background reading on the ultradian diet includes:

De Marinis, L., Folli, G., D'Amico, C., Mancini, A., Sambo, P., Tofani, A., Oradei, A., and Barbarino, A. (1988) Differential effects of feeding on the ultradian variation of the growth hormone (GH) response to GH-releasing hormone in normal subjects and patients with obesity and anorexia nervosa. *Journal of Clinical Endocrinology and Metabolism 66*(3), 598–604.

Jenkins, D., et al. (1989) Nibbling versus gorging: Metabolic advantages of increased meal frequency. *The New England Journal of Medicine, 321*(14), 929–935.

Mejean, L., Bicakova-Rocher, A., Kolopp, M., Villaume, C., Levi, F., Debry, G., Reinberg, A., and Drouin, P. (1988) Circadian and ultradian rhythms in blood glucose and plasma insulin of healthy adults. *Chronobiology International 5*(3), 227–236.

Spencer, H. (1990) *The Women's Body-Rhythm Diet.* New York: Bantam.

Van Cauter, E., Desir, D., Decoster, C., Fery, F., and Balasse, E. (1989) Nocturnal decrease in glucose tolerance during constant glucose infusion. *Journal of Clinical Endocrinology and Metabolism 69,*(3), 604–611.

Wada, T. (1922) An experimental study of hunger and its relation to activity. *Archives of Psychological Monographs, 8,* 1.

CHAPTER 8 / The Ultradian Family

The technical literature on ultradians and family life includes:

Chiba, Y., Chiba, K., Halberg, F., and Cutkomp, L. (1977) Longitudinal evaluation of circadian rhythm characteristics and their circaspetan modulation in an apparently healthy couple, in J. McGovern, J. Smolensky, and A. Reingerg (Eds.), *Chronobiology in allergy and immunology* (pp. 17–35). Springfield, IL: Charles C. Thomas.

Dinges, D., and Broughton, R. (1989) *Sleep and Alertness.* New York: Raven Press.

Ellis, L., and Ames, A. (1987) Neurohormonal functioning and sexual orientation: A theory of homosexuality-heterosexuality. *Psychological Bulletin, 101*(2), 233–258.

Feher, S., Berger, L. Johnson, J. and Wilde, J. (1989) Increasing breast-milk production for premature infants with a relaxation/imagery audiotape. *Pediatrics, 83,* 57–60.

Olness, K., and Conroy, M. (1985) A pilot study of voluntary control of transcutaneous PO by children: A brief communication. *The International Journal of Clinical and Experimental Hypnosis, 33*(15), 1–5.

Olness, K., Wain, H., and Ng, L. (1980) Pilot study of blood endorphin levels in children using self-hypnosis to control pain. *Developmental & Behavioral Pediatrics, 1*(4), 187–188.

Rudman, D., Feller, A., Nagraj, H. et al. (1990) Effects of human growth hormone in men over 60 years old. *The New England Journal of Medicine, 323,* 1–6.

CHAPTER 9 / The Synchrony of Love

Scientific background reading on the ultradian-circadian/sexual connection includes:

Kleitman, N. (1982) Basic rest-activity cycle—22 years later. *Sleep, 5*, 311–315.

Kupfer, D., Monk, T., and Barchas, J. (1988) *Biological Rhythms and Mental Disorders.* New York: Guilford.

Rose, K. (1988) *The Body in Time.* New York: Wiley & Sons.

Rossi, E., and Cheek, D. (1988) *Mind-Body Therapy: Ideodynamic Healing in Hypnosis.* New York: W. W. Norton. (Detail on women's consciousness and sexuality.)

Sapolsky, R. (1990) Stress in the wild. *Scientific American,* January, 116–123.

Sapolsky, R., and Ray, J. (1989) Styles of dominance and their endocrine correlates among wild olive baboons. *American Journal of Primatology,* 1–13.

Veldhuis, J., and Johnson, M. (1988) Operating characteristics of the hypothalamo-pituitary-gonadal axis in men: Circadian, ultradian, and pulsatile release of prolactin and its temporal coupling with luteinizing hormone. *Journal of Clinical Endocrinology and Metabolism,* 67(1), 116–123.

Veldhuis, J., King, J., Urban, R., Rogol, A., Evans, W., Kolp, L., and Johnson, M. (1987) Operating characteristics of the male hypothalamo-pituitary-gonadal axis: pulsatile release of testosterone and follicle-stimulating hormone and their temporal coupling with luteinizing hormone. *Journal of Clinical and Endocrinological Metabolism,* 65, 65–929.

CHAPTER 10 / Many Paths, One Goal

General aspects of a unified theory of consciousness and healing would include:

Belenky, G., Sing, H., Thomas, M., Shepanek, N., Hall, D. and Zurer, J. (1991) Ultradian rhythms in cognitive performance. (In Press.)

Kleitman, N. (1963) *Sleep and Wakefulness as Alternating Phases in the Cycle of Existence.* Chicago, IL: University of Chicago Press.

LaBerge, S., and Rheingold, H. (1990) *Exploring the World of Lucid Dreaming.* New York: Ballentine.

Lavie, P. (1985) Ultradian rhythms: Gates of sleep and wakefulness, in Schultz, H. and Lavie, P. (Eds.), *Ultradian Rhythms in Physiology and Behavior.* New York: Springer-Verlag.

Redmond, D., Sing, H. and Hegge, F. (1982) Biological time series analysis using complex demodulation, in F. Brown and R. Graeber (Eds.), *Rhythmic Aspects of Behavior* (pp. 429–457.)

Rossi, E. (1972/1985) *Dreams and the Growth of Personality.* New York: Brunner/Mazel.

Rossi, E. (1990) The eternal quest: Hidden rhythms of stress and healing in everyday life. *Psychological Perspectives, 22,* 6–23.

Rossi, E. (1990) The new yoga of the west: Natural rhythms of mind-body healing. *Psychological Perspectives, 22,* 146–161.

Rossi, E. (1990) Mind-Molecular Communication: Can We Really Talk to Our Genes? *Hypnos, 17*(1), 3–14.

Rossi, E. (1990) From mind to molecule: More than a metaphor, in J. Zeig and S. Gilligan, (Eds.), *Brief Therapy: Myths, Methods and Metaphors.* New York: Brunner/Mazel.

Rossi, E. (1990) The wave theory of consciousness: Creating a new mind-body therapy. Paper presented at Second International Evolution of Psychotherapy Conference, Anaheim, CA.

Rossi, E. (1991) The wave Nature of consciousness. *Psychological Perspectives, 24,* 1–10.

Schultz, H. and Lavie, P. (Eds.). (1985) *Ultradian Rhythms in Physiology and Behavior.* New York: Springer-Verlag.

Wever, R. (1979) *The circadian system of man.* New York: Springer-Verlag.

Wever, R. (1989) Light effects on human circadian rhythms: a review of recent Andechs experiments. *Journal of Biological Rhythms, 4,* 161–185.

White, L., Tursky, B. and Schwartz, G. (1985) *Placebo: Theory, Research and Mechanisms.* New York: Guilford.

Research in Los Angeles comparing meditators and subjects high in hypnotic susceptibility is reported in:

Rossi, E., and Cheek, D. (1988) *Mind-Body Therapy: Ideodynamic Healing in Hypnosis* (page 46). New York: W. W. Norton.

The scientific literature on the relationships between ultradian rhythms, meditation, and the relaxation response includes:

Benson, H. (1975) *The Relaxation Response.* New York: Avon.

Benson, H. (1983) The relaxation response and norepinephrine: A new study illuminates mechanisms. *Integrative Psychiatry, 1,* 15–18.

Benson, H. (1983) The relaxation response: Its subjective and objective historical precedents and physiology. *Trends in Neuroscience,* July, 281–284.

Holmes, D. (1985) To meditate or simply rest, that is the question: A response to the comments of Shapiro. *American Psychologist, 40,* 722–725.

Holmes, D. (1987) The influence of meditation versus rest on physiological arousal: A second examination, in M. West (Ed.), *The Psychology of Meditation* (pp. 61–103). Oxford: Clarendon Press.

INDEX

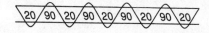

Abaissement du niveau mental, 7–8
Accessing and creative reframing,
    77–81
  defined, 78
  method of, 78–79
Accessing questions, 75
Accidents, fatigue-related,
    111–113
Activity(ies)
  importance of, for seniors,
    154–155
  shifting, 103
Adaptability, 30, 31, 37, 59, 86,
    153, 162
Addiction(s)
  eating as, 129
  hormonal high and, 39
  pregnancy and, 143–144
  Ultradian Healing Response
    and, 137–139
  Ultradian Stress Syndrome and,
    137, 138
Adolescents, 141, 152–153, 163
Affirmations, 65
Aging, 19, 153–154
Air-traffic controllers, 111
Alertness, 19, 90
  basic rest-activity cycle and, 28
  midafternoon-evening dip in,
    98–99
  morning-midafternoon, 98–99
Anxiety, 44
Appetite regulation, 121–126.
    See also Eating behavior
Armitage, Roseanne, 98

Aserinsky, Eugene, 22
Athletics, 116–119
  interval training, 117–119
  maximizing performance in,
    116–119
Autonomic nervous system, basic
    rest-activity cycles of, 23–24
Awakening, 76–77
  sexual synchronicity and, 166
  after Ultradian Healing
    Response, 56–57

Babies, 145–146
Basic rest-activity cycle (BRAC),
    10, 22–24. *See also*
    Ultradian rhythms
  activity phase, 11
  chronic disruption of, 38–39,
    43–44
  genetic basis of, 26
  hormones and, 23–25
  lack of awareness of, 51–52
  length of, 59
  need for self-healing and, 50–51
  nighttime dreams and, 61
  rejuvenation phase, 11–12, 13,
    26–27, 28–29, 30, 64. *See
    also* Ultradian Healing
    Response
  scheduling work/classes and,
    91–92
Bellisle, Dr., 131
Benson, Herbert, 178
Biofeedback, 13

Biological rhythms, 14–29. *See also*
    Circadian rhythms;
    Infradian rhythms;
    Ultradian rhythms
Births, 161
Blood sugar levels, 124
Bodily activities, and ultradian
    rhythms, 22–24
Bonding
    parent-infant, 145–146
    of sexual intimacy, 165–176
    synchronized ultradian rhythms
        and, 87, 106, 141, 144,
        145–146
Brain. *See also* Mind/brain
        functions
    breathing and, 81–85
    testing hemisphere balance
        of, 82
Brain-breath connection,
        81–85, 172
Breaking point, 21
    defined, 98
    managing, 98–100
    recognizing, in families, 151
    Ultradian Healing Response
        and, 99–100
Breaks, need for, 10. *See also*
        Ultradian Healing
        Response
Breastfeeding, 144–145
Breathing
    brain hemisphere activity and,
        81–85, 172
    deeper, accessing, 52–54
    patterns of, shift in, 52–53
    ultradian rhythms and,
        81–85, 172

Care-giving professionals,
        110–111
Charcot, Jean-Martin, 6, 7, 9
Children. *See also* Families
    parent-infant bonding,
        145–146
    ultradian eating plan for,
        123–124
Cholecystokinin (CCK), 126

Cholesterol levels, 19
    and ultradian hourly eating, 128
Chronobiology, 1
Churchill, Winston, 20–21
Circadian rhythms, 17–21
    daily activities and, 19–21
    defined, 15
    entrainment of, 85–89
    of seniors, 154
    sexual desynchrony and,
        168–169
    of sexuality, 162–164
    twenty-five hour cycle of, 168
    ultradian rhythms and, 17–19,
        98, 142
    weight control and, 131–133
Clerical workers, 109
Cognitive style, and basic rest-
        activity cycle, 98
Common everyday trance, 4–6, 64
    patterns of behavior during, 5, 7
    therapeutic process and, 5
    ultradian rhythms and, 11–12
Computer workers, 109
Consciousness, states of. *See also*
        Common everyday trance;
        Unconscious mind
    altered, 62, 63
    natural variations in, 3, 4, 7, 9
Creativity/creative work, 8, 9,
        60–61
    basic rest-activity cycle
        and, 28
    border states of consciousness
        and, 9
    optimum time of day for, 20
    Ultradian Healing Response
        and, 108–109
    writing down ideas and,
        97–98, 102
Cyclin, 26

Daily rhythms. *See* Circadian
        rhythms
Dating, 170–171
Daydreaming, 60, 61–62, 96
Daytime, 20–21
Dement, William, 120

Depression, psychological, 41–42, 137
Diary, ultradian, 68–69, 71–73, 83, 85, 132
  survey form, 189
Dieting, ultradian approach to, 123, 126–128, 130
Dissociation, therapeutic, 74
Distancing behaviors, 149
Dream period, 17, 19, 23, 61
Drugs, and Ultradian Stress Syndrome, 39
Dysrhythmia, low-amplitude, 93

Eating behavior, 67, 121–137
  entraining through, 86–87, 127, 148
  physiology of, 124–126
  synchronizing rhythms through, 87
  ultradian principles of, 121–124, 126–128
  uncontrolled, 45, 128–130, 132–133
Endocrine system. *See also* Hormones
  basic rest-activity cycles of, 23–24
  mind-body communication and, 24–25
Endorphins, beta-, 39, 129
Energy level, and circadian rhythms and, 17, 19
Entraining, 53, 94, 179
  eating and, 86–87, 127, 148
  hypnosis and, 180
  jet lag minimization through, 87–89
  parent-child synchrony, 147–149
  psychosocial, 86
  of ultradian and circadian rhythms, 85–89
  ultradian sychronicity and, 147–149, 166–167
  utilizing, at work, 105–106
Environment, facilitative, 50, 59
  for work, 104–105

Erickson, Milton H., 1–6, 11–12, 53, 80–81
Escapism, overeating as, 129–130
Estrogen levels, 134
Evolution, 30, 161

Families. *See also* Babies; Children
  dependent behavior in, 150
  distancing behaviors in, 149
  recognizing breaking point in, 151
  self-nurturing in, 151
  ultradian rhythms and, 140–159
  Ultradian Stress Syndrome and, 149–150
Fantasizing, 67, 163, 173–174, 179
Fatigue
  accidents and, 107, 111–113
  chronic, 32
  negotiation meetings and, 114–115
  overeating and, 129
  after ultradian break, 67
Fetal alcohol syndrome, 143–144
Fetuses, ultradian rhythms in, 142–144
Flexibility. *See* Adaptability
Flow state, 94
Food, as entrainer, 86–87, 127, 148
Foreplay, 175
Freud, Sigmund, 6, 8, 179
Friedman, Stanley, 43

Gastrointestinal disorders, 44–45
Genes, 25–26
Genetic clocks, 15, 17
Glucose levels, 116
Gregory, Bruce, 106
Group projects, 94
Growth hormone, 19, 45
  for seniors, 156
Growth-hormone releasing hormone (GHRH), 45

Halberg, Franz, 16, 46
Hawking, Stephen, 108

Headaches, 72
Healing, systems of, 177–182
    holistic, 13, 63–64, 70,
        178, 179
Healing and relaxation periods,
    Erickson's observations of,
    2–6. *See also* Ultradian
    Healing Response
Heart problems, 45, 112
Herser, Rex, 16
Hitchcock, Alfred, 171
Holistic approaches to health,
    13, 63–64, 70, 178, 179
Home-based workers, 110
Hormones
    activity high and, 37–39
    chronic stress and, 36–39
    female, 161–162
    male, 162–163, 164
    mind-body communication
        and, 24–25
    and suppression of need for
        rejuvenation, 38–39, 40
Hunger, ultradian rhythms of,
    67, 121–126
Hyperactivity, and hormones,
    37–39
Hypnosis, 7, 8, 9, 180–181
Hypnotherapy, 13, 53, 86
    Erickson's work with, 1–6
    Ultradian Healing Response in,
        180–181
Hypothalamus, 122

Imagery, 13, 54, 64, 179
Immune system
    basic rest-activity cycle and, 24
    chronic stress and, 33, 43
    melatonin and, 19
Industrial production workers, 107
Infradian rhythms, 15, 16–17,
    161–162
Insights, 4, 60–61
    awakening and, 20
    creative, 60–61
    daydreams and, 62
    dreams and, 62
    healing periods and, 4

in psychotherapy, 180
    Ultradian Healing Response
        and, 55, 96
Insulin, 124, 135–136
Intuition, 56

Janet, Pierre, 6, 7–8, 9, 41
Jenkins, David, 128
Jet lag, minimizing, 87–89
Jung, Carl G., 6, 9, 62

Kaufmann, Elizabeth, 117
Klein, Raymond, 98
Kleitman, Nathaniel, 22, 24,
    91–92
Kobayshi, Toshinori, 98

Larks, 19, 20
Left brain hemisphere, shift to, 97
Levie, Peretz, 98–99
Libet, Benjamin, 60
Liburd, Rosemary, 132
Life review process, 155
Life span, and stress, 45–46
Limbic-hypothalamic system, 37
Lippincott, Brian, 144–145,
    157–159
Lunch hour, 97

Managers, ultradian-enlightened,
    104–106
Meaning synthesis, 155
Meditation, 62, 63–64, 70, 130,
    177, 181
Meetings, 95–96
Melatonin, 19, 161
Memory, 19, 40–41
    of seniors, 156–157
Men
    circadian rhythms of, 162–163
    monthly rhythms of, 16
Menstrual cycle, 15, 16
Messenger molecules, 24–26
Mind-body messages, of need for
        rejuvenation, 5, 24–25,
        26–27
    adolescents' awareness of, 152
    ignoring, 50–51, 108, 137

learning to believe, 50–52
recognizing and facilitating,
    35–37, 48–49, 68, 70, 71,
    73–74, 96, 114
spontaneity of, 73–74
symptoms as, 78
of Ultradian Stress Syndrome,
    35–46
Mind/brain functions
genes and, 25–26
hormones and, 223–25
ultradian rhythms and,
    22–24
Mini ultradians, 101
Mistakes, 40–41, 93
Monthly rhythms, 16–17
sexual activity in, 160
weight control and, 134–136
of women, 161–162
Mood, and circadian rhythms,
    17, 19

Napping, 55. *See also* Sleep
in afternoon, 156, 156
controlled, 111
in morning, 155
versus Ultradian Healing
    Response, 63
Nasal balance, 81–85, 96
Negotiation
occupations involving,
    113–115
ultradian suggestions for, 115
Night owls, 19, 20
Nighttime, 19–20, 21
Nursing mothers, 144–145
Nurturance
in families, 151
self-, 50–51, 110–111, 151
Nurturing professions, 111

Obsession-compulsive thought, 36
Occupations, ultradian-related
    considerations for, 106–113
Office, ultradian, 104–105
Oral needs, ultradian rhythm of,
    121, 122
Overeating, patterns of, 128–130

Overweight, and circadian
    rhythms and, 131–132

Pain control, 72
through accessing and creative
    reframing, 78–80
Parasympathetic nervous system,
    53, 82
Parent-child synchrony, 145–149
Peak performance, 23. *See also*
    Performance
maximizing, 93–100
planning for, at work, 92–100
shifting, 95–96
Performance. *See also* Peak
    performance
in athletics, 116–119
basic rest-activity cycle and,
    10, 26–29, 98
individual variation in, 105
in industrial production, 107
monthly rhythms and, 15
peak, maximizing, 93–100
postprandial dip in, 20
society's demands for, 31
Ultradian Stress Syndrome and,
    40–41
Pert, Candace, 25, 104
Pilots, 111
Placebo response, 179
Plant rhythms, 15
Pregnancy, Ultradian Healing
    Response during, 142–144
Problem solving, 74–77
Progesterone, 134–135
Psychoanalysis, 179
Psychosomatic symptoms, 32–33
Ultradian Stress Syndrome and,
    42–46
Psychotherapy, 179–180
Public health and safety, 111–113

Questions
accessing, 75
ultradian, 74–77

Rainis, Arlene, 135–136
Receptive states, 76
Erickson on, 2–6

Recognition of signals of need for
    rejuvenation, 35–37, 48–49,
    68, 70, 71, 73–74, 96, 114
  ignoring, 50–51, 108, 137
Reframing, creative. *See* Accessing
    and creative reframing
Rejuvenation. *See also* Ultradian
    Healing Response
  awakening and, 56–57
  innate need for, 30–32
  mind-body rhythms and, 54–55
  recognition of need for, 35–37,
    48–49, 68, 70, 71, 73–74,
    96, 100–101, 114
  suppressing need for, 36–37,
    38, 39, 40, 43–44, 50–52, 93
Relaxation Response, 178
Relaxation techniques, versus
    spontaneous ultradian shifts,
    73–74
Right brain hemisphere, 97
  nursing and, 145
  sexual intimacy and, 163, 172
  shifting to, 81, 96, 103
  Ultradian Healing Response
    and, 54
Rosenthal, Norman, 136

Sampolsky, Robert, 164
Scheduling, of work, 91–92, 95
Seasonal affective disorder (SAD),
    16–17, 136–137
Seasonal rhythms, 14–15, 16–17,
    136–137, 161–162
Self-employed workers, 110
Self-esteem, 41–42
Self-nurturance, 50–51,
    110–111, 151
Self-regulation
  basic rest-activity cycles of,
    23–24
  mind-body rhythms of, 14–29
  suppressing need for ultradian
    breaks and, 44
Self-talk, 51, 76
Selye, Hans, 43
Seniors, 141, 153–159
  activity necessary for, 154–155

enhanced sexual intimacy
    for, 176
  growth hormone for, 156
  memory of, 156–157
  naps for, 155–156
  quest for meaning, 155
  sleep problems of, 157–159
  youthfulness of, 156
Sexual intimacy
  desynchrony and, 168–170
  discovery weekends for,
    167–168
  enhancing, with Ultradian
    Healing Response, 165–176
  touch and, 174–175
Sexuality
  circadian rhythms of, 162–164
  rhythmic basis of, 160–176
  seasonal rhythms of, 161–162
  seniors and, 176
  socialization and, 164–165
  stress and, 163–164
  ultradian rhythms of,
    162–163
Shamanism, 177, 178–179
Shift-workers, 112–113
Sleep. *See also* Napping
  psychomotor performance and,
    111–113
  and restoration, 65
  stages of, 17, 22
  ultradian break and, 67
  disturbances of, 157–159
  in seniors, 157–159
  Ultradian Stress Syndrome
    and, 44
Spatial skills, 27–28
Spontaneity, 73–74
Stress, 8, 10, 23, 30–46, 79.
    See also Ultradian
    Stress Syndrome
  chronic overactivity and, 12
  hormones and, 36–39
  overeating and, 128–129
  sexuality and, 163–164
  psychosomatic illness and,
    42–46
Suggestibility, 41, 179, 180

Suggestions, 75–76
auto-, 65, 77
versus accessing and creative
reframing, 79
Survey, 183–189
Sympathetic nervous system,
53, 82
Symptoms, as guides to healing, 78
Synchrony, ultradian, 87, 106, 144
parent-infant bonding and,
145–146
of sexual rhythms, 160–176

Take-a-break signals, 35–37,
48–52, 101
unconscious response to,
101–102
heeding, 35–37, 48–49, 68, 70,
71, 73–74, 96, 100–101, 114
ignoring, 31–32, 36–37, 38, 39,
40, 43–44, 50–52, 93
Teenagers. *See* Adolescents
Telephone operators, 109–110
Television viewing, 66–67
Therapeutic process, 5, 179–180
Touch, and sexual intimacy,
174–175
Twenty-minute break. *See*
Ultradian Healing
Response

Ultradian Healing Response,
8, 12–13, 36, 47–69.
See also Take-a-break
signals
active type of, 101–102
alternatives, 100–103
benefits of, 56–57, 60–62, 69
common questions about,
63–68
discovery of, 1–13
for eating problems and weight
control, 121–139
experimenting with, 66, 69
facilitating entry into,
50, 57, 59
first after awakening, 20
four stages of, 48–57

heeding signals for, 35–37,
48–49, 68, 70, 71, 73–74,
96, 100–101, 114
intensive on, 68–69
length of, 59, 63–64
mini-, 101
versus napping, 63
neglect of, 31–32, 36–37, 38,
39, 40, 43–44, 50–52, 93
number needed per day, 65
seniors and, 153–154,
156–157, 158–159
sexual intimacy and, 165–176
stage one of (Recognition
Signals), 48–52, 58, 74
stage two (Accessing the Deeper
Breath), 52–54, 58, 74–76
stage three of (Mind-Body
Healing), 54–56, 58,
60–61, 76
stage four of (Rejuvenation and
Awakening), 56–57, 58,
76–77
starting to practice, 67–69
stress symptoms and, 12–13
Survey, 183–189
tools to increase potential of,
70–89
Ultradian questions, asking, 74–77
Ultradian rhythms, 22–24. *See also*
Basic rest-activity cycle;
Ultradian Healing Response
bonding through
synchronizing, 87, 106, 144,
145–146, 160–176
circadian rhythms and,
17, 98, 142
consequences of ignoring,
30–46
defined, 15–16
discovery of, 9–10
entrainment of, 85–89
flexibility of, 30, 31, 59
graphs and charts of, 11, 12
modifying, 95–96
parallels between rhythms of
body and mind, 11
peaks and troughs of, 11

Ultradian rhythms, *continued*
  pioneer work in, 6–9
  of seniors, 153–154
  sexual desynchrony and,
    169–170
  of sexuality, 162–164
  society and, 31–32
Ultradian Stress Syndrome, 93
  addictions and, 137, 138
  awareness of, in families,
    149–150
  breaking spiral of, 46
  family problems and, 149–150
  four stages of, 34–46
  negotiating skills and, 114
  seniors and, 153–154
  stage one of (Take-a-Break
    signals), 35–37, 58
  stage two of (High on
    Hormones), 37–39, 58
  stage three of (Malfunction
    Junction), 39–42, 58
  stage four of (Rebellious Body),
    42–46, 58
  symptoms of, 32–34
  white-collar workers and, 108
Unconscious mind, 60, 75
  windows into, 3–4, 6, 11, 66,
    162, 180

Verbal skills, and basic rest-activity
  cycle, 27–28
Vigilance, 111–113
Visualization, 178. *See also*
  Imagery

Walking breaks, 66–67, 101, 103
Ward, Ann, 117
Weight control, 122–123, 125,
    126, 128–137
  circadian rhythms and,
    131–133
  monthly rhythms and, 134–136
  seasonal rhythms and, 136–137
White-collar workers, 107–109
Windows into unconscious mind,
    3–4, 6, 11, 66, 162, 180
Work, 90–115
  ideal ultradian conditions for,
    103–106
  scheduling ultradian breaks at,
    93, 95, 97, 99–100, 102
  Ultradian Healing Response
    and, 65–66, 90–115
Workaholics, 38
Workday, typical, 91

Zen, 177, 178, 181